Educational Policy-Making and the State Legislature

Mike M. Milstein
Robert E. Jennings

The Praeger Special Studies program—utilizing the most modern and efficient book production techniques and a selective worldwide distribution network—makes available to the academic, government, and business communities significant, timely research in U.S. and international economic, social, and political development.

Educational Policy-Making and the State Legislature
The New York Experience

Praeger Publishers   New York Washington London

PRAEGER SPECIAL STUDIES IN U.S. ECONOMIC, SOCIAL, AND POLITICAL ISSUES

Library of Congress Cataloging in Publication Data

Milstein, Mike M
     Educational policy-making and the state
legislature.

     (Praeger special studies in U. S. economic,
social, and political issues)
     Bibliography: p.
     1. Education—New York (State).   2. New
York (State) Legislature.   3. Education and state
—New York (State).   I. Jennings, Robert E. ,
joint author.   II. Title.
LA337. M55   379'. 152'09747   78-185780

PRAEGER PUBLISHERS
111 Fourth Avenue, New York, N.Y. 10003, U.S.A.
5, Cromwell Place, London SW7 2JL, England

Published in the United States of America in 1973
by Praeger Publishers, Inc.

Printed in the United States of America

This book was written to enhance understanding of the educational policy-making process at the state level. Though limited to New York State, the findings should have significant implications for the process of educational policy-making throughout the United States. The interactions and dynamics portrayed in New York State can be found, given appropriate consideration for idiosyncrasies and traditions, in all of the states.

The debate that has raged in educational circles over the propriety of looking at educational policy-making as political in nature seems to be abating. With resistance waning it is becoming legitimate to conceptualize education as a proper arena for political study. The present work is thus simply one more in a growing list of studies that document the political nature of education. Once the rear-guard battle being fought by educational purists is defeated, we can get on with the critical task of understanding the educational policy-making process. Such understanding is absolutely vital if educators are to exercise leadership in bringing political resources to bear on the needs of education. If educational leaders do not choose to play such a dynamic role, it is certain that others will play it for them with less than optimal results for education and the youngsters served by educational systems.

The primary audience for this study is thus the educational community. It is intended that as a result of reading this book educators will have a better understanding of the interactions that take place in the policy-making process and feel more confident about playing active roles in that process themselves.

This study is also addressed to political scientists. For too long political scientists have tended to shun education as a viable arena for the study of policy development. It is hoped that this volume and others like it will provide an impetus for behavioral scientists to move into this relatively virgin territory and shed some much needed light on the process.

We analyze educational policy-making from the viewpoint of formal government, but include any and all actors who play roles in the process as relevant members of the policy-making system. Thus, while the state legislature emerges as the central arena of policy interactions, the behavior of interest groups, educational government structures, and the office of the state governor are viewed as integral elements in the policy-making process. The few recent studies that have explored educational policy-making at the state level have, in the main, tended to look exclusively at the activities of actors outside of the state legislature, or, in a few instances, exclusively at activities within the state legislature. A central purpose of the present volume is thus to construct a bridge between two polar analytical perspectives.

We are indebted to many people who have helped to make this study possible. In particular we are indebted to the New York State Office of Education and to Leon Cohen who, as assistant professor of political science at the State University of New York at Albany, cooperated with us in our research. We also appreciate the coordinative roles played in the study by Thomas Henstock, Henry O'Donnell, and Willa Reister. Finally, we acknowledge the patient reconstruction of our notes and the typing of our manuscript by Jean Sullivan and Pat Martin. If there are errors in the presentation they exist despite the good efforts of these people and are the sole responsibility of the authors.

Buffalo, New York

Mike M. Milstein
Robert E. Jennings

CONTENTS

LIST OF TABLES

LIST OF FIGURES

Educational Policy-Making
and the State Legislature

1

POLICY-MAKING
AND EDUCATION

This work centers upon state government, in which people, groups, and organizations dependent upon state treasuries to further their objectives compete for the allocation of scarce resources. The roles and interactions of those who attempt to influence this process will be evaluated in this study. Participants include both those within formal state government and those whose business it is to monitor and affect the conduct of these formal actors. In short, this study is an exploration of the process that ultimately leads to decisions concerning "who gets what, when, and how."[1] Specifically, it reports the results of a study of the educational policy-making process in New York State.* Its findings, with appropriate recognition given to unique contextual differences, should provide insights into analysis of the educational policy-making process in other states. In this chapter the reader will find a general introduction to the problem, an initial perception of interactions that take place in the policy-making process, and a summary of research questions and methodologies employed in the study.

EDUCATION AND THE POLITICAL PROCESS

Education makes great demands on the public treasury, accounting for approximately 35 percent of all local and state public

---

*Robert E. Jennings and Mike M. Milstein, <u>Educational Policy Making in New York State with Emphasis on the Role of the State Legislature</u>, Department of Health, Education and Welfare, Office of Education, Small Grants Program Project No. 9-8-030, December 1970.

expenditures.[2] Yet education has not until recently been thought of as a topic for political study. In large part this neglect is due to the fact that educators have shunned attempts at political analysis of their institutions, insisting that education must remain above politics. Educators have argued that the intellectual independence of the educational structure can be maintained only if it is kept free of politics.

The myth that the schools must be kept out of politics has been a long-standing tradition in the United States. The myth was created by shrewd mid-nineteenth century educators who convinced the public and politicians of the sanctity of education and their own position as the best judges of how much of the public's resources should be allocated to the educational process and how these resources should be employed. They operated the educational system with little external influence. Given the low level of political structures in the nineteenth century,[3] the schoolman's desire for a protective barrier between educational institutions and politics is understandable.

The nineteenth-century educator built a protective web around his domain. Societal conditions, however, were radically different from those encountered by the educator of today. Educators no longer have complete command of the field, for their activities have increasingly come under intensive scrutiny by non-educators. Economists, for example, have defined the portion of the public dollar devoted to education as a well-placed and potentially high-return investment in human capital.[4] Education, vital to our technological society, is sought after by increasingly broader sectors of the population.[5] With the redefinition by economists and broader citizen involvement, laymen and politicians alike are climbing over education's ivy-covered walls more closely to scrutinize activities within. While most laymen no longer accept the myth that schools must be kept out of politics, twentieth-century educators seem to have come to believe it. As Laurence Iannaccone notes, the schoolman's "loss of touch with reality [is] a self-seduction, which is the most dangerous form of fascination."[6]

Our Federal System and Education

Public education, probably more than any other government-sponsored institution, is one of the most thoroughly political enterprises in American life. Partisans of public education are active competitors in the allocation of scarce resources. The peculiarities of the system of support for education in the United States make this true at all levels of government. In 1970 public education received 52 percent of its support from local sources, 41 percent from state sources, and 7 percent from federal sources.[7]

4

At the local level political processes in education thrive. The school board, the elected or appointed group of laymen responsible for overseeing the school district's educational programs and finances, is selected by political processes. When school boards and educational administrators request community approval of bond issues and annual budgets they employ political processes. Curriculum controversies and racial segregation or integration are but three of the many educational issues that require consummate political skills on the part of educational leaders. In a growing number of urban and suburban communities a new element has been added to the already complex policy-making structure. School boards and educational administrators in these communities are being confronted with issues of regional cooperation, issues that tend to divide citizens throughout metropolitan areas into warring camps.

At the state level partisans of public education must compete with other government-sponsored sectors as they seek to impress governors, legislators, and agency heads with the legitimacy of their demands on state resources. Educational issues debated in policy-making centers of state government include the amount of general aid to be allocated to education and the formula by which that aid will be distributed, categorical aid programs such as urban aid and reading programs, curriculum matters such as mandatory subjects to be taught and textbooks to be used, professional certification requirements, and state legislation concerning collective negotiations for teachers.

At the federal level Congress has begun to respond affirmatively to the needs of education. The definition of the federal government's role in public education is still disputed and unclear, but there is little question that the demands for federal involvement are increasing. The federal share of fiscal resource inputs for education increased from 4.4 percent in 1960 to about 7 percent in 1970.[8] Some students of educational governance predict that the federal share "over a period of years" might rise as high as 33 percent.[9] As the federal share rises, educators, quite appropriately, are attempting to influence the direction of federal involvement to meet the needs of public education most effectively.

Because of its resource needs education is inextricably drawn into the policy-making process. It is through this process that it is decided which educational programs will be pursued and at what levels they will be supported. Resource allocation decisions are made in a highly competitive governmental area. Those who participate in the process, therefore, must be highly organized and fully comprehend the process of public policy-making—both formal and informal—to assure favored treatment of their interests. Necessary continued support of education can be assured only by skillful involvement of educational leaders.

A Critical Arena:
State-Level Educational Policy-Making

Study of the educational policy-making process at the state level is of particular contemporary importance for several reasons.

First, while responsibility for education has long been accepted as a state function, it is only recently that states have begun to allocate increases in their level of support for education. Most states have at least kept pace with the increasing financial needs of education; some are interpreting state-level responsibility for education even more broadly. The increased dollar input of 23 states between 1960 and 1970 actually outpaced the increased input from local sources, the traditional support base. For example, state support increased from 31.9 percent to 43.2 percent in Idaho and 37.8 percent to 46.4 percent in New York in that decade.[10]

Second, many state legislatures and governors have begun to interpret their roles in educational policy-making as active rather than passive. Educational decision-making is becoming centralized within state legislatures and governors' offices. Further, this centralization has been occurring at an accelerating rate. Such concern for the policy-making initiative, noted as early as 1960 in California,[11] is beginning to be felt in other states. This can be seen in efforts by state legislatures to increase specialized staff personnel, to scrutinize proposals, and, occasionally, to originate legislative programs for such special problems as urban aid and school district consolidation or decentralization.

Third, as the states increase their resource inputs and centralize their policy-making processes, educational interest groups (e.g., administrator organizations, school board organizations, teacher organizations, and various education-related citizens' organizations) increase their state-level activities, clamoring for education's "fair share" of state resources. In the past educational interest groups have generally been able to impress state legislative bodies with the "special" nature of education. Today they find significant resistance to their demands. One reason is that it is becoming increasingly difficult for teachers, administrators, and school boards to work together.* Another reason is that the expanding role of state governments in an ever broadening definition of public responsibility

---

*Where, in the past, these interest groups were noted for the close working relationships they maintained, the noted feature today is disintegration of coalitions. This is largely related to the increasing tempo of teacher militancy, which is driving school boards and administrator groups apart from teacher groups. (See Chapter 6.)

for "soft areas" such as medical care, unemployment insurance, and other social welfare programs is bound to have an eroding effect on the support of public education. Both factors—the splintering of educational interest groups and increasing demands for public dollars—have much to do with the accelerating pace of state government initiative in educational policy-making.

Finally, few scholars have explored this vital government policy-making area. Until recently education, especially at the state level, has not been thought of as an area for study in terms of politics, the process from which policies emerge. As late as 1959 a student of politics was able to note that education is a political entity, "a fit subject for study—yet neither educators nor political scientists have frequently engaged in examination of public education from this angle."12 Partially filling the void were three books published in the early 1960s. Stephen K. Bailey et al. (1962), Michael Usdan (1963), and Nicholas A. Masters et al. (1964) scrutinized the power of educational interest groups at the state level.13 Each work examined the structure of educational organizations, the means of coalition-making, and the ways in which educational interest groups exert influence on state governments. The processes of policy-making within the formal structure of government, however, were of no concern to Bailey or Usdan and only of passing interest to Masters. John C. Wahlke et al. and Ferguson have studied the policy-making process within the formal government structure, but their interests extended well beyond education and their analyses were confined to depth surveys of legislative bodies at the state level.14

This study attempts to fill gaps left by these studies. It will explore the policy-making behavior of those within state government, including the educational governing board, the state education agency, the governor, and the legislature. It will also examine strategies employed by interest groups as they attempt to influence state officials and the perceptions of policy-makers concerning the effectiveness of these strategies.

New York State is the setting of the study, but the results reported and the models derived should be useful for analysis of educational policy-making in other states. The tendency of the New York State legislature to play a central role in education finds parallels in other states. For example, in a study of the educational policy-making process in the California State legislature between 1957 and 1965, Laurence J. Fahey notes increasing partisanship in voting patterns and a tendency to centralize educational decision-making within the legislature itself.15 Tom Wiley, observing the same tendency in New Mexico, notes that "it appears that the legislature is strongly committed to do the major research and make the command decisions in determining educational needs and support, using professional people in an exalted 'choreboy' role. . . ."16 Iannaccone, reviewing available reports of state educational policy-making across the country, concludes that legislatures will become major initiators in educational policy-making.17

Why has centralization of educational decision-making within legislative bodies been occurring in states as geographically separate and demographically different as California, New Mexico, and New York? Some factors appear to be common to all three states. These factors include increasing fragmentation of educational interest groups, making it more difficult for educators to "speak with one voice" when dealing with state legislators and governors, resource requirements in education that are increasing at a faster rate than the general economy, more knowledgeable state legislators as rewards for participating in state government are increased, greater representation of urban and suburban areas in state legislatures as a result of the Supreme Court's one man—one vote reapportionment decision in Baker v. Carr,18 and, in general, an increasing interest by citizens and public officials in the methods and results of public education.

These factors exist to one degree or another in all 50 states. Thus it is certainly possible that states in general might be moving toward increasing centralization of educational policy-making within their state governments. If this presumption has foundation, the results of the present study should be of more than passing interest to educators, political scientists, and state officials. As noted earlier, however, due consideration to unique historical, geographic, and demographic variables must be given when applying findings of the present study to other states.

THE POLICY-MAKING PROCESS:
AN INITIAL PERCEPTION

Policy-making might be viewed as a cycle involving movement from unsatisfactory conditions to greater satisfaction with conditions. This cycle—which can be referred to as a Present-Preferred Cycle—includes the following stages:

A. Period of Dissatisfaction. Specific groups (e.g. blacks, women, youth, the aged, labor) become unhappy with constraints upon their activities. This might be due to the existence of oppressive policy or lack of desired policy.

B. Reformulation of Attitudes. If dissatisfaction is great enough, some new direction and crystallization of attitudes take place. Leaders emerge and are given—or take—responsibility to articulate the group's grievance.

C. Idea Formulation. The original negative criticism of the aggrieved group is translated into alternatives to the constraining situation. These alternatives might come from others enlisted in the cause.

D. Debate. The scope of involvement is widened to enhance the potential of successfully "selling" alternatives. This process makes active participants (and potential supporters) out of latent critics and encompassing necessary modifications in proposed alternatives before they reach the legislative stage.

E. Legislation. The formal mechanisms of government are petitioned to move alternatives into law. (Government officials are usually involved in the policy process long before it gets to this stage.)

F. Implementation. The new law must be put into effect. This becomes the responsibility of executive agencies.

The cycle is fraught with high-risk situations. The policies that emerge on the implementation end of the cycle are but a fraction of those that are proposed at the dissatisfaction end. Even these few policies are usually severely modified by the weathering of time, expediency, challenges by other policies, and harassment by the opposition. Nor is the process static. Modified laws or new laws are open to challenges by groups that feel disadvantaged by them. In short, the cycle often begins anew as groups are constantly forming around dissatisfactions.

The portion of this process that is of particular concern to the study is the legislative stage. It is at this point, as Harold Lasswell would say, that "who gets what, when, how" is decided. This is the vital linking point at which demands are processed through negotiation strategies of cooperation, bargaining, and competition between and among interest group leaders, state education agency officials, legislators, and the governor.

Individuals and groups who are not members of the legislature but who are involved at the legislative stage can be defined as those "interacting with legislators, sometimes . . . [with] other outsiders—and when the purpose of this interaction is related to the legislative process."[19] For our purposes, individuals, groups, and organizations can be thought of as involved in the legislative stage when their actions are directly related to the process of educational decision-making at the state level.

Malcolm E. Jewell and Samuel C. Patterson present a useful visual construct of membership composition at the legislative stage.[20] (See Figure 1.) The individual groups and organizations within the peripheral circles can act independently or in various combinations upon the legislature to affect alternatives under consideration. Such activity is highly complex and often subterranean. Peripheral groups are not necessarily involved throughout the entire process. They

9

might enter and leave the process at various stages, depending on whether they see advantages in involvement or noninvolvement. Further, only a portion of these groups' efforts are centered on the legislative process. For example, educational administrators and state education agency officials become part of the system when their activities are focused on affecting educational policy-making at the state level but not when they are dealing with the day-to-day running of schools. Similarly, the governor and his officers are part of the system when their activities have implications for the direction of public education in the state.

FIGURE 1

Legislative System Configuration

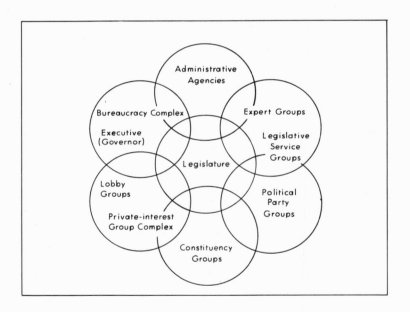

Source: Malcolm E. Jewell and Samuel C. Patterson, The Legislative Process in the United States. New York: Random House, 1966, p. 6. (Reprinted by permission.)

Problem and Research Questions

The constructs presented above led to the original formulation of the problem to be studied and also helped to clarify research questions that needed answers. The major purpose of the research was to analyze the process of educational policy-making in New York State. The focus was upon the role of formal government structures—in particular, the state legislature. How that role is perceived by interest group leaders, the Board of Regents, State Education Department officials, the governor, and state legislators sets the parameters and methodological procedures to be used in the study. Contrasts and comparisons of these perceptions were of particular interest to ascertain implications for future educational policy-making activities at the state level in New York.

Methodological procedures and data analyses were guided by research questions that focused on the roles of the legislature, the governor and his offices, the State Education Department, the Board of Regents,* and educational interest groups.

The first understanding that must be established is the way the legislature goes about processing its tasks, especially those tasks related to educational questions. Second, to complete the linkage, how the legislature is influenced in this processing activity by the governor, the Board of Regents and the State Education Department, and educational interest groups must be added to the knowledge base. How the various groups interact in the development of educational policy becomes the focus of analysis.

A. <u>The legislature</u>. How does the legislature treat educational policy issues? Pursuant to this question it becomes important to ascertain if education legislation is treated the same as other legislative matters, whether education matters are viewed as politically viable (i.e., lead to rewards such as advancement in the legislature or secure needed votes for retention of office), and whether party membership dictates positions taken on educational legislation. Related questions include: Does the legislature take the initiative in educational policy development? Is there extensive legislator expertise in this policy area and are there able back-up staff and sufficient information available to legislators for rational decision-making? As they go about developing educational policy, to what

---

*The State Education Department and the Regents, New York's State Board of Education, for analysis purposes, are held separate from the governor and his offices. This is due to the unique position of the Board of Regents and the State Education Department in New York State. This point will be discussed in Chapter 5.

extent and in what manner do legislators interact with other state government officials such as the governor and his officers, the State Education Department and the Board of Regents, interest group representatives, and their constituents? Finally, what effects do contextual factors such as teacher militancy, the general state of the economy, and the differing needs of New York City and upstate New York have upon the processing of educational legislation?

B. The governor and the executive agencies. What role does the governor play in the legislative process? To what extent can he bring influence to bear on the legislature as the highest state officer who represents the entire state? What mechanisms does the governor have at his disposal for influencing the legislature's educational decision-making? To what extent is he viewed in the legislature as the leader of his party? Does his veto power affect legislative outcomes? Does his executive budget, which is formulated before the legislative session begins, have an impact on legislative activity? Do executive agencies such as the budget office and other planning offices influence legislative activity? Finally, do special state commissions and their recommendations influence legislative activity?

C. The State Education Department and the Board of Regents. What mechanisms are at the disposal of the State Education Department and the Board of Regents for influencing the legislature's educational decision-making? Does the Board of Regents' unique position as a public policy agency for all educational activities at the state level put it in a favorable policy-influencing position? How does the department employ its extensive expertise in developing information for presentation to the governor and the legislature? What types of relationships are established with educational interest groups to advance preferred legislative proposals? What access do the department and the Board of Regents have to the governor and the legislature? What strategies do they use in attempting to obtain favorable legislation?

D. Educational interest groups. What strategies are employed by interest groups in attempting to influence legislation? How do they attempt to influence the legislature directly? How do they attempt to influence the legislature indirectly—e.g., through the governor, the State Education Department, local officials, and the news media? What resources can they bring to this task? Do they cooperate with each other to influence legislation? Have teacher militancy and collective negotiations affected cooperation among educational interest groups?

Methodology

The setting of the study was the state capital, Albany. The study was timed to coincide with the 1969 session of the state legislature. Relationships among and between the role groups were analyzed as the session unfolded and educational policy-making progressed. Followup of the state's educational policy-making through 1972 is also included in the analysis.

To answer the research questions posed, four research methods were employed: document search, unstructured interviews, structured interviews, and an in-depth survey. Document search was carried out to help establish the initial definition of the problem. Documents were explored to help researchers identify the critical activities and actors in the policy-making process. Documents utilized included political party platforms, legislative committee reports, legislative regulations, bylaws, resolutions, public statements, proposed legislation memoranda, hearing transcripts, and interest group publications. Document search was continued through the course of the study to verify, modify, and otherwise help shape the analysis.

Unstructured interviews were then held with individuals within both the government and the interest group leadership who were identified through document search as critical role-players in the policy-making process. The interviews were conducted to expand upon the knowledge gained in document search and to further specify the parameters of the study. They helped to clarify the meaning of documentary materials and to place in a clearer prospective the critical participants in the legislative process. Those interviewed included selected interest group leaders, legislative counsels, and officials in the Division of the Budget, the Office of Planning Coordination, and the State Education Department.

On the basis of data gathered through document search and unstructured interviews, a sharper focus for the study was constructed. Structured interviews with interest group leaders were then carried out to ascertain their influencing strategies and their perceptions of the legislative process as it concerns educational matters. These perceptions were later checked against those of legislators to determine the extent of perceptual congruence between these two groups. Structured interviews were conducted with members of the executive staffs who were <u>officially</u> responsible for the lobbying activities of the following organizations:

> Citizens Public Expenditure Survey, Inc.
> Conference of Large City Boards of Education
> Conference of Mayors, New York State
> Educational Conference Board of New York State—
>   (Conference Board) (ECB)
> New York Council of School District
>   Administrators (NYCSDA)
> New York State School Boards Association (<u>NYSSBA</u>)
> New York State Teachers Association (<u>NYSTA</u>)
> United Teachers of New York (UTNY)

To establish perceptions of legislators, an in-depth survey instrument, portions of which were adapted from Wahlke, et al.,[21] was developed. Of New York's 207 state legislators (150 assemblymen and 57 senators), 117 complied with the request for a substantial time commitment to respond to the survey instrument (90 assemblymen and 27 senators). This represents a 57 percent response (60 percent of all assemblymen and 47 percent of all senators). Legislators interviewed were all men with a median age of 43.7 years and a median length of service of 3.8 years in the state legislature. Fifty-one percent were Democrats, 48 percent Republican and 1 percent "other."* Most legislators characterized their districts as metropolitan areas—60 percent urban, 25 percent suburban, 10 percent rural, and 5 percent from mixed demographic areas. The resultant information was coded, programmed, and processed at the State University of New York at Buffalo.

To accomplish the purposes of the study the following time sequence was observed:

1. September—October 1968. Review of the literature, identification of primary role players, schedule of appointments with legislators, committee staff members, and officials in the executive branch, and attendance at annual meetings of several state educational organizations.

2. November—December 1968. Review of historical support for education in New York State, document analysis, interviews with legislators and other state officials centering on the approaching legislative session, identification of issues, design of survey instruments.

3. January—March 1969. Observation of activities, continued interviews with government officials and interest group officials during the legislative session, attendance at committee meetings and hearings.

4. April—June 1969. Interviews with legislators.

5. June 1969—February 1970. Followup on results of the legislative session with state officials and interest group representatives.

---

*Comparable figures for the total 1969-70 legislature follow: There were four women in the legislature in 1969-70. For the 67 percent of legislators whose dates of birth were listed in their official biographies, the median age was 46.5 years. The median length of service for all 207 members was 3.9 years. The legislature was controlled by the Republicans; 78-to-72 in the assembly, 33-to-24 in the senate.

6. March 1970—December 1970. Collation and analysis of data gathered with some replication of steps two and three above, writeup of initial findings.

7. January 1971—June 1972. Continued analysis of educational policy-making at the state level.

Organization of the Book

This book is organized around the major groups involved in the educational policy-making process. Chapter 2 explores the setting of the study. The next four chapters present views of each actor group as well as the interrelationships among the groups in the policy process. Within these chapters brief historical sketches, the current outlooks of the various groups, and their perceptions of the legislative process, as determined by observation and interviews, will be analyzed. Chapter 3 focuses on the state legislature, Chapter 4 on the governor, Chapter 5 on the Board of Regents and the State Education Department, and Chapter 6 on the educational interest groups. Chapter 7 presents two case studies as illustrations of how these groups interact in the educational policy-making process. Chapter 8 provides a summary and synthesis, drawing implications for future directions of educational policy-making at the state level.

2

The broad socio-economic-political setting within which educational policy-making takes place has a bearing on the results obtained and the processes by which they are derived. A diversity of societal demands on education creates a diversity of demands and counter-demands on the state's policy system. Wealth is important in creating a good educational system and it is being recognized increasingly that a sound educational enterprise is essential to economic growth. The societal expectations and economic well-being of a state, in turn, bear on its political outlook. Policies that affect education are fashioned on the anvil of the state's social and economic condition; political traditions in state-local relationships are the hammer.

NEW YORK: A SUPERSTATE

The term "Empire State," applied to New York, is not a booster's facile phrase. Since the Civil War when the state's economic base shifted from agriculture to industry, New York has usually led the other states in production, population, and income.* At the same time the economy of New York State has enjoyed stability through its diversified nature.[1] In 1970 its population was 17.9 million. Its work force totaled 7.1 million. Of this number over 1.8 million people were employed in manufacturing, 1.2 million in government, 1.9 million in finance and service, and 1.5 million in wholesale and retail trade. Farming employed 122,000 people. Per capita income averaged

---

*It was not until the 1960s that California replaced New York as the nation's most populous state.

$4,797, the highest in the nation. These data can be compared with those of other populous states (see Table 2.1).

The reasons for New York's preeminence are several. Located in the middle Atlantic region on the eastern seaboard and stretching inland almost to Ohio, the state has proximity to both raw materials and ready markets. Nearly 85 million people in the United States and Canada live within a 500-mile radius of Syracuse, New York. There has always been an abundant supply of labor in a population expanded by migration from surrounding states and by immigration. Since colonial times New York has been a banking center, supplying capital for growing businesses. Cheap transportation by water, rail, and highway, has also contributed to the state's development.

Much of the Empire State's industries and businesses are concentrated in the New York City area, the urban centers of the Hudson and Mohawk river valleys, and the eastern shore of Lake Erie. New York City, with its Long Island and Westchester suburbs, is the nation's center for manufacturing, fashion, finance, marketing, and transportation. The concentration of labor, capital, markets, and services in this area is without parallel in the world.

Halfway up the Hudson River Valley, as it stretches north from New York City almost to Canada, the cities of Albany, Schenectady, and Troy form another metropolitan concentration. Electronic and

TABLE 2.1

Population, Employment, and Income:
the Five Most Populous States
(1970)

| State | Population (thousands) | Employment (thousands) | | | Per Capita Income (1970 est.) |
		Manu-facturing	Finance and Service	Wholesale and Retail Trade	
N.Y.	17,979.7	1,883.9	1,907.1	1,510.2	$4,797
Calif.	19,696.8	1,608.2	1,537.0	1,537.6	$4,469
Pa.	11,663.3	1,549.3	815.0	846.0	$3,893
Tex.	10,989.1	764.5	734.8	978.1	$3,515
Ill.	10,973.9	1,377.5	857.5	952.7	$4,516

Source: 1970 County Business Patterns (Employment), Per Capita Income from 1971 Statistical Abstract of the United States.

electrical equipment, papermaking, and metal fabrication are major industries of the region. The Mohawk River joins the Hudson near Albany and now, as in colonial times, the capital area is a transportation crossroads for the upstate region and New England to the east. Westward through the Mohawk Valley to the Great Lakes, the city of Amsterdam, the merging metropolitan area of Rome-Utica, and the cities of Syracuse and Rochester are all centers of manufacturing. Products range from carpets and wire to cameras and sweaters. On Lake Erie, a gateway to middle America, are Buffalo, Niagara Falls, and Lackawanna, forming an urban sprawl with concentrations of heavy industry and electro-chemical production. Buffalo is also a major Great Lakes port.[2] Agriculture still plays a sizable role in the business of the state. Farming in the river valleys and the uplands is diversified, with dairying, truck farming, grape-growing, and the raising of livestock providing the largest income.

Within this superstate there is a supercity, New York. Its immense size is heightened by comparison with the other 61 cities in the state. There are over eight million people in New York City, sixteen times the number in the state's second largest city, Buffalo, which has just under one-half million population. New York City's budget was $6.87 billion in 1971, more than ten times the combined budgets of the next five largest cities in the state and larger than that of a majority of the states. There are more Italians in New York City than in Rome, more Jews than in Jerusalem. Nearly 55 percent of the population are blacks and Spanish-surnamed Americans. There are 1.1 million public school pupils, nearly one-third of the state's total enrollment. The City accounts for 50 percent of the state's employment and over two-thirds of its economic activity, measured in dollars. In any consideration of New York State, therefore, the City usually must be given separate attention. The reason for this will become more apparent in later chapters.

New York State will continue to hold its position as a superstate. Its geographic location astride transportation and communications lines, its diversified businesses and industries, and its resultant wealth form a solid base for future growth. The wealth of New York has established it as a superstate. The politics of the state are commensurate with that status, yet not completely congruent with it, as the next section will demonstrate.

THE POLITICAL MAKEUP OF NEW YORK STATE

There are three levels of activity and aspiration in New York State political life. At the national level many New Yorkers have played major roles. As the spotlight of national political fame sweeps the stage, New York politicians find it tempting to bathe in its glare. Then there is local politics. Town, city, and county, offering sufficient challenges and rewards for many aspirants, reflect a strong tradition of political localism. National and local politics meet at the state level, specifically in the legislative and executive branches of state government as they seek to develop programs to solve state-wide problems. The mix provides a starting point for controversies—e.g., over whether a policy decision was made to improve conditions within the state or to further someone's image on the national scene. It also provides a basis for the rural-urban-suburban divisions in New York politics.

National, State, and Local Politics

The politics of a superstate cannot fail to be bound up with the politics of the nation. Given New York's century and one-half as the leading state of the union, these bonds have been built up and reinforced in every election. The governorship, U.S. Senate seats, or residence and business affiliation in New York provide springboards for drives toward the presidential nomination of both major parties.[3] Franklin D. Roosevelt planned his career in a straight line from state senator through the governorship to the White House. Thomas E. Dewey and Nelson A. Rockefeller utilized the office of the governor extensively in their presidential nomination bids. Robert F. Kennedy went to great lengths to become a U.S. Senator from New York to have a better base when he sought the presidential nomination. Dwight D. Eisenhower established himself as a Republican through his brief residence in the state before becoming a presidential aspirant. Richard M. Nixon, who was once thought to be all through in politics, established New York residence immediately after his defeat for the governorship of California and went on, of course, to a successful comeback. These examples leave little doubt that chances for national office are enhanced by being part of New York's political or business life.

Many of these men contributed to New York's growth and development. Each of the three governors mentioned provided leadership and programs to better the state. Roosevelt started a "Little New Deal" at the outset of the Great Depression—a program continued by his successor, Governor Herbert H. Lehman. Dewey gave fiscal responsibility a new meaning by pointing out that it wasn't how much the state spent that was important but on what it was spent. Dewey's programs for housing and reemployment of returning World War II veterans were among the best in the nation. He also expanded the state's participation in slum clearance projects and highway improvement. Rockefeller has gone on in this vein, attacking the larger social ills of the cities and waste in human and natural resources. Under Rockefeller new programs of crime and narcotics control have been introduced. He has also taken steps to provide more public recreation areas and to check water pollution. But these men and other governors who harbored lesser ambitions have had to struggle against an almost inborn localism in state government. In spite of the state's size, wealth, and long involvement on the national level, politics in New York State might still be characterized largely as town-and-county "court house politics."

Local government in New York State is a hybrid of early New England town government developed into a county-township system. Local control and distrust of centralized executive power are traditions of this system. These traditions are still embodied in "home rule" provisions in the state constitution and in statutes as bulwarks against state domination of local affairs. Under home rule proposed changes in the structure or function of local governments must be approved by voters in the affected jurisdiction. Thus the state government, seeking to solve state-wide problems, has had to utilize the carrot of financial or other aid to wield a subtle stick to obtain cooperation by local governments. Many a local politician goes to Albany on a record of fighting state control "to help the folks back home" by taking a seat in the legislature. Town, city, and county offices provide places in which aspirants to state office can begin practicing the political arts.

The strength of local governments and suspicions of executive power are reflected in state government. The legislature has historically been a meeting place in which local interests are furthered. This has been done at the expense of state-wide interests and often at the expense of other localities. In particular, rural towns and counties have benefited at the expense of the cities reflecting some traditional splits and sections in New York politics.

Splits and Sections

There are political splits and sections in all states. American politics has long lived with them and, indeed, fostered them down to this century. The upstate-downstate split in Illinois and the east-west divisions in Tennessee and Kentucky are built on urban-rural dichotomies. The north-south split in California is based on scarcities of water in the south and people in the north. In Connecticut it is the Connecticut River Valley and its industry against the rest of the state and its rural villages. In New York it is an upstate-downstate split compounded by rural, suburban, and urban divisions.[4]

Sectionalism in New York politics is part and parcel of localism and has three ingredients: the geographic upstate-downstate split, a dichotomy of urban and rural populations, and party politics, particularly Republican politics.

The Upstate-Downstate Split. The upstate-downstate split is not as clear a set of divisions as the term would indicate. Downstate in New York City and Democratic by political persuasion with a more than three-to-one margin in party enrollment. The rest of the state, from New York City east to the tip of suburban Long Island and north through suburban Westchester to Canada and west to Buffalo, is upstate and Republican. But there are inconsistencies in this pattern. The City has downstate suburbs, too; three of its five boroughs, Manhattan, Queens, and Staten Island have strong Republican enclaves. The Republican edge in suburban Long Island is a little over 50 percent by party enrollment and there are strong Democratic areas upstate near the Canadian border, in the City of Buffalo, and in some of the smaller cities.[5] Still, a state-wide or national Democratic candidate must come up with a sufficient voter majority in New York City to overcome voting deficits in the upstate areas and carry the state.

The Rural-Urban Dichotomy. The rural-urban dichotomy is a variation of the upstate-downstate split; cities tend to be Democratic, the countryside Republican. As in most of the northeastern United States, city people are largely unionized workers. Ethnic groups—Italian, Irish, Black—are concentrated there. Catholics and Jews are major religious groups. These people are most often Democratic voters. Rural people are most often white Anglo-Saxon Protestant middle class farmers and merchants and Republican. In New York, however, this doesn't begin to explain solidly Republican upstate cities like Rochester, Schenectady, and a half dozen others in the industrial Mohawk Valley. It also ignores the fact that rural New Yorkers make up only 14 percent of the state's population while the suburbs, which constitute 35 percent of the population, go essentially unaccounted for in this variation. Republicans have held the countryside, however, and used it as their political base since the early 1900s.

Republican Domination. Governor Alfred E. Smith, a Democrat, once said that New York is constitutionally Republican, thus expressing the fact that domination of rural New York provided Republicans with the means of dominating the state. As in other states the rural cast of politics has been extended from the agricultural past into the post-industrial present. In New York a "chameleon effect" permitted the Republicans to hold the rapidly filling suburbs in the years following World War II. People moving out of the cities into suburban towns often switched from Democratic to Republican as protective coloration. Through Republican control of the legislature redistricting remained a party matter; New York's cities were sliced like pies so that the suburbs and rural areas provided the bulk of voters in many districts. Thus, with state-wide Republican enrollment of 3 million voters to the Democrats' 3.6 million, the GOP held both houses of the legislature and all but one of the four state-wide elective offices in the executive branch in 1969, the year of this study.

Splits and Sections Illustrated

Two Elections. Two recent gubernatorial elections illustrate these points as well as the growing exceptions. In 1966 the incumbent governor, Republican Nelson Rockefeller, won a third term, defeating William O'Connor, a Democrat and New York City district attorney by some 400,000 votes out of 6 million cast. In 1970 Rockefeller was returned for a fourth term over Democrat Arthur Goldberg, a former U.S. Supreme Court Justice and Ambassador to the United Nations, by 700,000 votes out of 6 million. (See Tables 2.2 and 2.3.)

In both elections there was also a Conservative party candidate—an ideological departure from the usual Conservative endorsement of the Republican. The Liberal party put up a separate candidate in 1966 but returned to its practice of endorsing a "suitable" Democrat in 1970*

In 1966 Rockefeller ran on his two-term liberal record and in the face of hostile reaction to the state's first sales tax, which he had imposed two years earlier. In 1970 he moved more toward the right of center in discussing the issues. The Democrats in both elections hit hard at the unmet needs of the cities as well as increasing crime, interracial problems, and rising state taxes and expenditures.

In 1966 Rockefeller lost New York City by more than 500,000 votes, but only two of its five boroughs. In 1970 he lost the City by almost 150,000 votes but won a plurality. These margins meant that

---

*The Liberal and Conservative parties in New York State each seek to pull the major parties toward more liberal or conservative stands. The Liberals, who won a place on the state ballot in 1946, have been successful through their ability to veto the choices of New York City Democrats who display leanings toward reenforcement of the status quo either politically or societally. The Conservatives, who won a place on the state ballot in 1962, essentially tried to emulate the Liberal party success by attempting to influence the GOP. While the two parties tend to cancel each other out in state-wide elections, the Conservatives have managed to influence a number of legislative elections to the extent that the Conservative viewpoint must be recognized by the Republican leadership.

TABLE 2.2

Vote for Governor in Selected Areas
of New York State, November 1966

Place	Republican Rockefeller	Democrat O'Connor	Liberal Roosevelt	Conservative Adams
New York City (five boroughs)	964,364	1,034,012	218,740	234,590
Nassau & Suffolk Counties (Long Island)	424,440	239,198	60,009	108,091
Westchester County cities	88,951	55,469	13,277	12,536
towns	105,389	31,980	11,420	15,110
Albany City	20,958	36,080	1,209	637
Troy City	12,795	11,839	1,336	530
Schenectady City	16,170	11,740	2,900	811
Amsterdam City	5,268	4,789	816	270
Utica City	14,010	16,424	3,096	1,491
Onondaga County Syracuse City	24,071	38,043	5,037	4,462
towns	32,158	44,536	6,969	9,331
Binghamton City	11,812	9,528	1,952	837
Watertown City	5,196	3,969	666	256
Ithaca City	3,473	1,977	556	300
Monroe County Rochester City	41,956	45,905	9,111	6,445
towns	70,339	44,056	12,943	16,089
Niagara Falls City	9,556	13,420	2,710	855
Erie County Buffalo City	53,856	94,645	15,522	5,974
other cities	4,797	9,986	2,210	685
towns	85,916	82,442	20,012	15,179
Jamestown City	5,620	5,011	1,314	698
Totals	2,001,095	1,835,046	391,805	435,177
Percent	42.9	39.3	8.4	9.3
Statewide Totals	2,690,626	2,298,363	507,234	510,023
Percent[a]	43.6	37.3	8.2	8.3

[a]Blanks, voids and scattered votes not included. Therefore, percentages do not total 100 percent.

Source: Secretary of State, New York State.

23

TABLE 2.3

Vote for Governor in Selected Areas
of New York State, November 1970

Place	Republican Rockefeller	Democrat Goldberg	Liberal Goldberg	Conservative Adams
New York City (five boroughs)	1,057,964	920,875	179,017	106,777
Nassau & Suffolk Counties (Long Island)	499,673	270,115	32,107	93,522
Westchester County				
cities	100,771	51,207	7,029	10,904
towns	118,065	45,629	6,576	12,001
Albany City	24,861	25,947	718	1,101
Schenectady City	17,913	9,686	403	1,647
Troy City	15,040	8,169	280	1,163
Amsterdam City	6,630	3,844	114	422
Utica City	20,208	11,283	300	1,619
Onondaga County				
Syracuse City	33,028	23,951	1,507	6,976
towns	54,566	30,487	1,642	15,649
Binghamton City	13,530	7,615	239	1,044
Watertown City	5,966	3,184	92	387
Ithaca City	3,677	1,857	392	320
Monroe County				
Rochester City	41,713	41,188	1,668	9,069
towns	84,453	56,176	2,301	24,274
Niagara Falls City	11,276	11,793	429	1,795
Erie County				
Buffalo City	53,995	85,412	3,381	7,771
other cities	5,907	10,111	355	1,230
towns	100,826	102,299	3,973	18,181
Jamestown City	6,627	6,219	174	784
Totals	2,276,689	1,727,047	242,697	316,636
Percent	49.9	37.8	5.3	6.9
Statewide Totals	3,105,220	2,158,355	263,071	422,514
Percent[a]	50.4	35.0	4.2	6.8

[a]Blanks, voids and scattered votes not included. Therefore, percentages do not total 100 percent.

Source: Secretary of State, New York State.

24

the Democrats in both elections had to do better than usual in upstate areas to make up the normal deficit.

In both elections the City's Long Island and Westchester suburbs, including six small cities, went to Rockefeller by nearly two-to-one. The Conservative party candidate did not appreciably cut into the usual Republican majority in these suburbs.

In 1966 Rockefeller lost traditionally Democratic Albany and Utica, but the eight or so small cities of the industrial Mohawk Valley remained traditionally Republican. In 1970 he lost Albany by only about 2,500 votes and won handily in Utica. Republican majorities in the other small cities were approximately the same as four years earlier.

Syracuse changed camps in 1966, going Democratic; more surprisingly, its suburbs did the same. Republican Rochester also gave the Democrats a majority but its suburbs went to Rockefeller. Syracuse and its suburbs returned to their Republican ways in 1970. The Conservative vote rose appreciably in 1970 but apparently did not affect the Republican effort. Rochester again gave the Democrats a slim majority but its suburbs went for Rockefeller with an 18,000-vote edge over Goldberg. The Conservative vote increased by one-third over 1966 but did not deny the governor a plurality in Monroe County towns.

In 1966 Buffalo joined the smaller cities along Lake Erie in the Democratic column while the Buffalo suburbs gave Rockefeller only a slim plurality. In 1970 the governor lost all of Erie County to his Democratic opponent, but the Conservative vote in the towns denied Goldberg a majority in the suburbs.

In short, New York State politics is changing. A liberal Republican, even one showing some conservative streaks, can now do well in New York City. There are fewer "safe" Republican areas, however. The large cities upstate are beginning to exhibit the same tendencies toward the Democrats as cities of comparable size in other parts of the industrial Northeast. The small cities seem to be remaining Republican with a few in the Democratic camp. The suburban areas, particularly the New York City suburbs, where the Republicans have built their strength, are still fairly reliable. A few upstate suburbs, however, are not as solid as the GOP might wish. The Conservative vote is cutting into their strength. This fact, coupled with the rise in Democratic voting, is causing concern in Republican party ranks.

Political divisions are slowly breaking down and so is Republican domination. Factors include court actions in line with the one man— one vote decision of the U.S. Supreme Court, a Conservative party moving out from under the GOP wing, and an increase in Democratic voting in the cities and suburbs.

SUPPORT OF PUBLIC EDUCATION IN
NEW YORK STATE

New York has moved from a financial structure in which the role of the state was supplementary to local school government to one that is, in principle, a state-local partnership in education. Progress toward universal free public education in New York is marked by two distinct periods of development. The first, from colonial times to 1900, was characterized by a largely local kind of education—the establishment and operation of schools by each community with the state prescribing minimal procedures. State funds were allotted to schools for partial support but the bulk of financing came from local sources. Following the turn of the century the state's role increased in both financing and prescription for operation. The major concerns of the state were to improve the quality of education in all schools, to extend educational opportunity to the less populated areas of the state, and to achieve equitable distribution of funds.

Development of Support

The basic pattern of education and its support was established in the years between the Revolution and the Civil War. Migrating New Englanders with their ideal of local self-government rooted out the Dutch-English tradition of aristocratic education. Used to tax supported common schools, they brought pressure to bear on the legislature. The result was the Common School Act of 1812, which provided for division of all towns into school districts, local school boards as agents of the state, a system of combined state and local financing, and a "Department of Public Instruction" headed by a state superintendent. The financial section of the act empowered local boards to levy taxes for school purposes, provided for state contribution to teachers' salaries, and allowed assessments against the parents of pupils (rate bills) to pay additional costs. In 1853 state support of secondary education began with the Union Free School Act, which provided financial incentives for consolidation of common districts to operate high schools.[6]

Improving educational opportunity and quality went hand in hand with financial support. Aid funds were paid to districts operating a school for six months. The number of children in attendance was also a factor. Quotas, set dollar amounts, were later added for each qualified teacher and supervisor. Money was collected through state taxes on real and personal property. Rate bills were abolished in 1867, leaving state and local tax systems to provide all school support. By 1900 the state was contributing 15 percent of the $263 million expended for public education.

The quota system became the means of allotting state aid between 1900 and 1925. Additional provisions and dollar amounts for each teacher, supervisor, and maintained class were voted almost yearly as the legislature tried to keep up with the expansion of schools. By 1925 a patchwork of 25 different bases for aid distribution made up an uneven and unfair system of state support. State contributions had slipped to 8 percent of a total expenditure for schools of $283 million.

In 1925 the Cole-Rice Act established the equalization principle. Aid was distributed on the basis of teacher units of pupils in the local school, less an allowance for the taxable wealth of the district: the less taxable wealth, the greater the aid amount. The act also provided transportation and building aid for rural districts that were reorganized into larger central districts. In 1927 the state's Friedsam Commission confirmed the equalization principle and recommended increased aid as tax relief. By 1930 the state's share of school support had risen to $100 million, 22.7 percent of the total expenditures for schools.[7]

The Friedsam formula remained the aid basis through 1944. Appropriations were reduced during the Depression of the 1930s but intensive lobbying by educational interest groups kept the legislature from abolishing the formula. School needs grew as the state's population grew and new programs were inaugurated.

In 1945 the foundation principle was adopted. Per-pupil allotments of aid dollars for toward a basic education program were grafted onto earlier acts providing equalization. Proposed increases in foundation program amounts became the focus of legislative struggles in succeeding years.[8]

State financial support of schools was changed to a shared-cost base in 1962. Under this concept the state shares in every dollar expended for education locally, the state share being determined by the value of property behind each pupil compared with the state's average value. Because the legislature was reluctant to make such a commitment in a single step a per-pupil aid ceiling was adopted. Aid amounts were increased by this legislation, but more important the shared-cost principle was accepted.[9] Through the succeeding years legislative activity has centered on efforts to raise the ceiling.

Current Support

State support for the public schools in New York has continued to increase steadily through the 1960s and 1970s. The level of state support and its financial effort have been consistently high compared with that of the other 49 states. Combined state and local expenditures for education are about $4.5 billion annually. The state's contribution climbed to nearly $2.4 billion in 1970-71 from $1.67 billion in 1967-68, keeping New York first among the 50 states in dollar amounts. (See Table 2.4.) On the average, state funds make up over 45 percent of public school revenues, reaching a high of 47.9 percent in 1970-71. State funds added to local funds, have kept the per capita expenditure for public schools at over $210, the second highest in the United States. (See Table 2.7.) New Yorkers contribute about 5.3 percent of their personal income to state and local revenues for schools. (See Table 2.6.)

New York with its 18 million people is second only to California in total population. In public school enrollment New York has 3.5 million pupils,* California 4.7 million. New York is first in dollar amounts of aid, California second. Sparsely populated Alaska ranks first, just ahead of New York, in per capita expenditure, however, while California is eighth. In terms of all school revenue New York State's contribution is 6 percent above the national average but only about half that of Hawaii with its single-district state system. Nearly half of New York's school revenues comes from the state level, placing the state New York seventeenth among the 50 states. (See Table 2.5.) The percent of personal income contributed to state and local school revenues in New York is high compared with the national average. (See Table 2.6.) Average personal income in the United States is $3,687, however, while in New York it is $4,442. Vermont ranks higher on this item, even though its personal income averages only $3,247.

New York State has consistently devoted large amounts of tax money to aid for local school districts. In terms of percentages nearly one-half of local school support comes from the state. Such a level of demand on the state's resources makes education a major consideration in the legislative arena.

Federal Aid in New York

The availability of federal funds for education since 1965 has been utilized by New York State largely in meeting the problems of city schools. By 1966-67, federal funds accounted for $211 million or 4.4 percent of all expenditures for public elementary and secondary schools in the state. With increases in state aid amounts, the percentage shrank to 4 percent in 1969-70. In that fiscal year federal monies to the state totaled $290 million of which $180 million were Title I funds for the education of disadvantaged children as defined in the Elementary and Secondary Education Act of 1965 (ESEA). New York

---

*Another 787,850 pupils were enrolled in New York's nonpublic schools. The vast majority, 663,850 (84.3 percent), were enrolled in catholic schools.

TABLE 2.4

TABLE 2.4

Estimated Public School Revenues from State Sources,
1967-68 through 1970-71: Selected States
(in billions of dollars)

State	1967-68		1968-69		1969-70		1970-71	
	Amount	Rank[a]	Amount	Rank	Amount	Rank	Amount	Rank
N.Y.	$1.67	1	$1.99	1	$2.12	1	$2.39	1
Calif.	1.23	2	1.26	2	1.42	2	1.47	2
Pa.	.75	3	.85	3	1.04	3	1.14	3
Tex.	.69	4	.70	4	.78	5	.98	4
Ill.	.47	5	.48	5	.82	4	.96	5
U.S. (average)	.24	-	.27	-	.31	-	.34	-

[a]Ranked by the authors

Sources: National Education Association, Estimates of School Statistics,
1968-69 (Washington: Research Division, The Association, 1968), p. 34 and subsequent publications of the same title for 1969-70, p. 34; 1970-71, p. 34; 1971-72,
p. 34. By permission.

TABLE 2.5

Estimated Percent of Revenue for Public Elementary and
Secondary Schools from State Governments, 1967-68 through
1970-71: Selected States

State	1967-68		1968-69		1969-70		1970-71	
	Amount	Rank	Amount	Rank	Amount	Rank	Amount	Rank
N.Y.	45.9	17	48.4	14	46.4	17	47.9	17
Calif.	34.7	28	33.9	31	37.3	27	35.2	30
Hawaii	83.2	1	85.1	1	87.2	1	89.4	1
Pa.	44.3	18	43.7	22	46.2	20	46.2	19
Ill.	28.0	38	26.6	41	34.8	33	38.2	25
U.S.	39.3	-	39.9	-	40.9	-	41.1	-

Sources: National Education Association, Rankings of the States, 1969 (Washington: Research Division, The Association, 1969), p. 47 and subsequent publications of
the same title for 1970, p. 46; 1971, pp. 48-49. By permission.

TABLE 2.6

Local and State Revenue for Public Schools as Percent of
Personal Income, 1967-68 through 1970-71: Selected States

State	1967-68 Percent	Rank	1968-69 Percent	Rank	1969-70 Percent	Rank	1970-71 Percent	Rank
N.Y.	5.1	12	5.4	8	5.3	15	5.8	18
Calif.	4.7	23	5.1	14	4.3	36	4.5	35
Vt.	6.2	2	5.7	6	6.5	1	7.4	2
Pa.	4.3	34	4.6	29	4.9	25	5.1	25
Ill.	3.9	43	4.2	38	4.7	29	5.3	22
U.S.	4.6	-	4.7	-	4.8	-	5.4	-

Sources: National Education Association, Rankings of the States, 1969 (Washington: Research Division, The Association, 1969), p. 46; and subsequent publications of the same title for 1970 p. 45; 1971 p. 47; 1972 p. 50. By permission.

TABLE 2.7

Per Capita State and Local Expenditures for Local Schools,
1967-68 through 1970-71: Selected States

State	1967-68 Amount	Rank	1968-69 Amount	Rank	1969-70 Amount	Rank	1970-71 Amount	Rank
N.Y.	$181.28	5	$218.56	2	$235.49	4	$300.00	5
Calif.	176.21	11	198.53	8	206.16	13	264.00	10
Alaska	226.30	1	225.76	1	292.20	1	341.00	1
Pa.	137.21	30	161.77	25	182.04	25	266.00	13
Ill.	141.99	26	160.19	27	182.36	24	216.00	29
U.S.	146.63	-	167.15	-	184.35	-	211.00	-

Sources: National Education Association, Rankings of the States, 1970 (Washington: Research Division, The Association, 1970), p. 57; and subsequent publications of the same title for 1971, p. 62; 1972, p. 62. By permission. U.S. Bureau of the Census, Statistical Abstract of the United States, 1972, p. 125.

City received 68.7 percent ($117.0 million) of that amount with some 266,468 pupils qualifying. The other ten largest cities, with a total of 180,886 qualified pupils, received $26.9 million of the remaining $53.3 million. For fiscal 1971-72 it was estimated that New York State received $196.3 million under ESEA titles and nearly $287.6 million from all other programs for elementary and secondary schools.[10]

The major concern of many legislators and educators is that New York does not get its fair share of federal aid. They point out that the federal government pays an average of 8 percent of school expenditures across the nation but only 4 percent in New York. Out of every $4 that New Yorkers send to Washington in taxes only $1 comes back in aid. The relative shrinkage of federal monies as a proportion of public school expenditures also indicates to New Yorkers that the federal effort is not keeping pace with the problems.

Federal aid channeled to cities is a cause of discontent in other school districts. State aid has increased but has not kept pace with costs and problems in rural and suburban schools. While ESEA Title III centers serve districts outside of cities and nonurban districts share in federal lunch programs and National Defense Education funds, these aids do not compare favorably with the amounts available under Title I, ESEA. The thrust of these districts has been to press for greater state funding while city districts lobby both in Albany and Washington.

* * *

The major elements of New York State policy-making have been presented, including the socio-economic strengths of the state, its political makeup, and the historical development of state support for education. A wealthy state, New York has been able to achieve a high level of financial aid for schools. A progressive state, it has sought improvement of education. The political setting in which these things have been accomplished has been outlined. The dominance of the Republican party, the upstate-downstate split, and rural-urban-suburban political divisions have been shown to be forces that act on the process.

The next step is to examine the policy process. Outside of the government structure are educational interest groups that seek to influence this process. Within the government structure there are three bodies that are central actors: the Board of Regents, the office of the governor, and the legislature. The Board of Regents is New York's unique, august, public policy agency supervising all educational activity in the state. The regents' staff arm is the State Education Department headed by the commissioner of education. The office of the governor includes the chief executive, his immediate staff, and 21 executive agencies—the Division of the Budget, the Office of Planning Coordination, and the regular line agencies. The legislature, the central focus of the study, is composed of the senate and the assembly. The next four chapters will focus on the roles in the policy process played by these groups, beginning with the role of the legislature.

3

THE STATE
LEGISLATURE:
FOCAL POINT OF THE
POLICY-MAKING PROCESS

The crucial choices among alternatives in the formulation of policy are made at the legislative stage, each group attempting to influence ultimate choices in directions that most closely meet the needs and desires of its constituency. For this reason the next four chapters will explore, group by group, the perceptions of the policy-making process and the tactics employed to influence that process.

In making its choices the legislature operates within a host of conditions inherent in its own structure. This chapter examines political parties and party control as well as the interrelationships of critical role positions within the legislature as they affect legislative operations. These role positions include the speaker of the assembly, the majority leader of the senate, and the committees in each chamber that are concerned with educational policy-making. Legislative power and role interrelationships will be cast in terms of the geographic, socioeconomic, and political dichotomies cited in Chapter 2. Of special interest will be the ways in which the legislature processes educational legislation. Included will be analyses of the level of knowledge of legislators concerning educational issues, educational policy-processing compared with processing in other substantive policy areas, sources of information available and used for decision-making, and sources of influence on legislators as they decide how to vote on educational legislation.

PARTY AND POWER IN THE LEGISLATURE

Legislative power in New York State is vested by its constitution in a senate of 57 members and an assembly of 150 members, all elected for two-year terms. Their power is extremely broad. The

legislature can do whatever has not been allocated to the United States
Congress by the federal Constitution. The legislature makes policies
for the state in the form of laws dealing with the broad range of social,
political, and economic affairs. It appropriates all state monies
and has the power of legislative oversight or review of the actions
of state officials. The only restriction on its power is a provision
in the First Amendment to the federal Constitution, a provision re-
peated in the bill of rights of the state constitution forbidding the
invasion of individual rights.

The legislature is specifically charged with responsibility in
education by article XI, section 1 of the state constitution: "The
Legislature shall provide for the maintenance and support of a system
of free common schools wherein all the children of this state may be
educated." This policy-making power, which has existed since 1895,
makes the legislature the focal point of the policy-making process
in education.

Legislative power is exercised to the accompaniment of the
clash of political parties. As Jewell has noted, politics is the key
to understanding American state legislatures.[1] Historically in New
York State this has largely meant understanding Republican party
politics, for the GOP has held the majority in both houses almost
continuously since 1874. For both major parties, moreover, control
of the legislature until the middle of this century meant control of
the state government.

Between the Civil War and the 1920s the legislature was the dominant branch of government. Through its power over appropriations it
controlled state programs and dealt with departments of government
to suit the political aims of the majority party. Strict party control
prevailed in the consideration of bills in committee and on the floor.
The legislative leadership, i.e., the speaker of the assembly and the
majority leader of the senate, exercised control through their chairmanship of their respective committees on rules and through the
power of appointment by the chairmen and members of other committees. Behind these leaders were the political bosses of the Republican or Democratic party. With control of patronage to encourage
party loyalty and election machinery that enforced party solidarity
at the local level the state leaders were kingpins in legislative politics. Legislators were caught between the party caucus and the
necessity of running for reelection at home. Legislative dominance
and party control are well illustrated by the statement (and actions)
of one party boss to a newly elected governor who showed signs of
independence: "You may be the governor but I have got the Legislature and the Legislature controls the governor and if you don't do
what I tell you to do I will throw you out of office."[2] The governor
did not comply and the party boss engineered his impeachment.

Governor William Sulzer was impeached in 1913 on orders from Democratic boss William Murphy.

Electoral and government reforms have eliminated the more blatant aspects of party domination of legislating, but it still remains an important consideration in the legislature. Jewell classifies New York State as one of nine in which the same party controlled both houses of the legislature but not the governorship between 1947 and 1962.[3] That one party was the Republican party with a rural power base and legislative control of reapportionment. The result of this domination has been a high degree of party discipline on both sides of the aisle. As Frank J. Munger observes, in New York "the Legislature of the the state possesses a party discipline far superior to that found either in the United States Congress or in all but a few state capitals. Almost all major issues are determined by party line votes; when dissenting votes are cast by party members they are ordinarily cast by permission of the party leaders."[4]

Republican legislators have essentially utilized party domination to enact the programs of Republican governors. This was particularly true during the administration of Governor Thomas E. Dewey (1943-54) when preponderant Republican majorities seemed almost to rubber-stamp administration proposals. When the Democrats controlled both houses for a brief period in the late 1960s they utilized their slim majorities to effect compromises with Republican Governor Nelson Rockefeller's programs. The ability of the majority Democratic party to dominate the legislative process forced a Republican governor to negotiate with the Democrats.

In the 1969 session the Republicans were in control with 78 of 150 seats in the assembly and 33 of 57 seats in the senate. Party domination was still evident. Of the legislators responding to this study survey 38 percent agreed that there was tight party discipline; another 16 percent felt that there was discipline depending on the issue at hand (see Table 3.1). Of those who felt that discipline was tight 45 percent believed that this discipline was possible because the leaders control internal patronage, rewards, and punishments. The leaders can also help or hinder the flow of bills and decide on committee assignments. Thirty-two percent of our respondents felt that discipline was the result of the common interests of party members rather than party control (see Table 3.2).

Most legislators acknowledged that they consider the views of their party leaders before voting on a bill but a majority (54 percent) tempered this consideration by saying that such deference to the leadership depends on other factors as well, (Table 3.3). Thirty-two percent noted that a critical factor in considering the party leaders' position is whether a bill is a party measure. Reciprocity was important to legislators who consider their party leaders'

35

TABLE 3.1

Party Discipline

Tight Party Discipline In N.Y. State Legislature	Total (N = 110)	Assembly (N = 85) (in percent)	Senate (N = 25)
Agree (Tight Discipline)	38	40	32
Agree, but Depends on Issues or Party	16	15	20
Disagree (Not Tight Discipline)	46	45	48
	100	100	100

Source: Compiled by the authors.

TABLE 3.2

How Discipline Is Maintained: Legislators Who Believe Discipline Is Tight[a]

How is Discipline Maintained?	Total (N = 44)	Assembly (N = 35) (in percent)	Senate (N = 9)
Power of Leaders/Internal Patronage/ Reward and Punishment/Committee Assignments	45	46	44
Party Conference and/or Caucus	14	11	22
Common Interest of Members of the Party (Ideological)	32	31	33
Personality of Leaders	2	3	—
Trade-Offs	16	17	11
Other	9	11	—

[a]Legislators gave multiple responses; therefore, columns do not total 100 percent.

Source: Compiled by the authors.

TABLE 3.3

Concern for Party Leaders' Positions on Bills

Consideration Legislator Gives to Party Leader Position on Bills	Total (N = 112)	Assembly (N = 86) (in percent)	Senate (N = 26)
Great Deal	27	26	31
Some Attention Along with Other Factors	54	58	42
Little or None	19	16	27
	100	100	100

Source: Compiled by the authors.

position (Table 3.4). As a result of considering the leaders' position, 41 percent of the respondents believed they in turn would get support for their own bills, while 25 percent thought they would have a better chance for promotion within the legislative system and 19 percent thought increased patronage and staffing privileges would be granted to them. In short, responding legislators were in agreement that party and legislative leaders are factors to be reckoned with.

Legislative Leadership

The direction of legislative power and the exercise of political discipline rest with the leadership—the officers and political party leaders in each house. Office and party are cojoined in that the temporary president of the senate is also the majority leader, and the speaker of the assembly are elected by majority vote along strict party lines.* Each office has extensive control over the organization and operation of the respective chambers. As such it becomes the jugular point for party control of the legislative process. The opposition party in each chamber elects a minority leader to represent it in the operation of the legislature.

---

*The majority party in the assembly also elects a majority leader whose tasks closely resemble that of the majority whip in the U.S. Congress. The majority leader is normally the hand-picked choice of the speaker.

The rules of each house give these legislative officers broad powers that can be used to control the legislature. In the assembly the speaker appoints all committee members and chairmen and is an ex officio member of each committee. He assigns bills to committees, appoints all legislative staff members, and controls the legislative budget. When joint legislative committees or state commissions are formed, the speaker appoints assembly members to them. His most powerful position, however, is chairman of the Rules Committee, which is made up of the majority and minority leaders and a number of other senior members from the majority party. The majority leader in the senate has a similar role.* He appoints all committees in the senate. As chairman of the Rules Committee he

TABLE 3.4

Advantages of Cooperating with Party Leaders[a]

Advantages of Going Along with Party Leader When He Seeks Your Support	Total (N = 103)	Assembly (N = 78)	Senate (N = 25)
	(in percent)		
None or Not Much	14	13	16
Support for My Own Bills	41	42	9
Patronage and Staffing	19	21	16
Further the Principles of Political Party (Ideological)	14	13	16
Promotion Within the System (Incl. Committee Assignments)	25	28	16
Support at Election Time/ Service to Constituents	10	9	12
Build Up Credit/Further Access to Information	6	6	4
Other	18	14	32

[a]Legislators gave multiple responses; therefore, columns do not total 100 percent.

Source: Compiled by the authors.

---

*The lieutenant governor is the presiding officer of the senate but acts only as a moderator.

has control of the flow of legislation. He also plays the role of floor leader for the majority party.[5]

The rules committees give the leadership the means to operate the legislative process to serve the needs of the majority party. In each house bills can be called in from other committees by the Rules Committee, which can report bills to the floor for immediate consideration. In the assembly all bills still under committee consideration two or three weeks prior to the close of the session revert to the Rules Committee at the call of the speaker and all other committees go out of business. Similar procedures obtain in the senate. The Rules Committee in the assembly consists of 22 members; in 1969 the majority party held 15 of these positions. In the senate there are five places on the Rules Committee but in practice most procedural decisions are made by the majority leader.

The committee system in the legislature has largely been an extension of the leadership. The most important committees are those that handle finance and appropriation measures. These are the Ways and Means Committee in the assembly and the Finance Committee in the senate. Each is chaired by a trusted lieutenant of the majority party leader. In all committees bills are assigned by the leaders, giving the chairman and majority membership firm control. In recent years the assembly has had 34 standing committees. But in the final analysis, as Stuart K. Witt reported, "about half of the committees had no control over any legislation considered significant enough for inclusion in the Speaker's summary of legislation and roll-call analysis. The Rules and Ways and Means Committees handled more significant legislation than all the rest of the committees together. And the Rules Committee almost completely dominated bills coming from the Senate."[6]

In 1969 there was some reform in the assembly with more bills, even those with financial implications, being sent to the substantive committees—such as education, social services—as well as to Ways and Means. An indicator of the increasing role of the substantive committees is the fact that in both 1969 and 1970 the standing committees were kept in business until very late in each session and many returned during the summer for briefings and planning sessions.

Leadership and Membership

The reins of party control can be drawn very tightly by the leaders when there is a need to reduce factionalism in a large majority or to help garner votes from the minority in a fairly evenly divided house. But the reins may not be drawn so tightly as to violate the informal norms of leadership conduct held by the members of the body.

In the assembly the speaker has usually held tight rein. In the 1940s Speaker Oswald Heck, with a large Republican majority, kept factional feuds at a minimum in order to assure passage of Governor Dewey's bills. Heck not only carefully regulated committee appointments and house patronage but kept many administration bills in the Rules Committee, even to the extent of ignoring the Ways and Means Committee on what he felt were crucial appropriations bills. In 1967 and 1968, when the Democrats held the lower house by a slim majority, Speaker Anthony Travia used the Ways and Means Committee staff to investigate financial requests made by Governor Rockefeller. Travia kept a close watch over money bills, assigning them only to substantive committees chaired by legislators he could trust. Otherwise key bills went to Rules or to Ways and Means. Travia's purpose was to force the Republican Governor to deal with a Democratic majority in the lower house and to have him press reluctant Republican legislators in both houses into endorsing compromise legislation.

When the Republicans returned to control in 1969 Speaker Perry Duryea began a legislative reform movement toward wider participation and greater responsiveness in the assembly. His first steps in this direction produced the immediate political result of helping to keep his slim majority of six together.[7] Eleven of this majority had been elected with substantial Conservative party support, so Duryea loosened the reins slightly. His purpose was apparently to keep conservative-leaning members content. Most were new to the assembly and less stringent control gave the speaker more room to maneuver.

In the senate Majority Leader Earl Brydges relaxed the tight control imposed by his predecessor, Walter Mahoney. Since 1966 Brydges has permitted the development of a more polycentric organization wherein committee chairmen have prerogatives independent of the party caucus.* Rather than utilize his staff to propose measures Brydges had them aid him in making judgments about committee decisions.

The manner in which the leadership wields its power is constrained by the norms of the membership. According to the survey, assemblymen tend to see the role of speaker in a way different from that in which senators see the role of the majority leader.

---

*Brydges formally announced his retirement at the end of the 1972 legislative session. His successor, Warren M. Anderson, has, as of this writing, demonstrated a bit more flair by hiring a speech writer and a press secretary. How he will operate the legislative organization remains to be seen.

TABLE 3.5

Roles of Speaker of Assembly
and Majority Leader of Senate[a]

Job of the Speaker and Majority Leader	Total (N = 117)	Assembly (N = 90) (in percent)	Senate (N = 27)
Sets Rules	18	21	7
Makes Legislative Staffing Appointments	16	18	11
"Runs the Show"	57	63	33
Looks After Interests of the Members	3	2	4
Controls the Party/States Party Position	38	33	59
Controls Committees (Appointments)	30	34	15
Controls Bills	30	32	22
Controls Finances	7	6	11
Resolves Conflict in the Chamber	9	7	15
Resolves Conflict in the Other Chamber	6	8	—
Resolves Conflict with the Executive Branch	4	4	4
Oversees the Governor's Program	9	6	16
Controls Debate on Legislation	10	10	11
Other	10	9	15

[a]Legislators gave multiple responses; therefore, columns do not total 100 percent.

Source: Compiled by the authors.

Assemblymen felt that the speaker "runs the show," that is, influences or tends to control all activities of the assembly. In the senate only about one-third of the respondents believed that the majority leader exercises this kind of control. Senators felt that the majority leader was the party spokesman more strongly than assemblymen felt that the speaker filled this role. Similarly, assemblymen more often than senators felt that their chamber's leader controlled the committees and the fate of bills. (see Table 3.5).

Returning to party discipline as a behavioral norm, some interesting views of leadership emerge. Of the 38 percent of respondents agreeing that party discipline was tight, less than one-half felt that this discipline was maintained because of the powers of the leadership, e.g. such powers as internal patronage, or committee assignments (see Table 3.2). Among those who said that party discipline was not tight, a third felt that this was so because neither the party nor the leadership was able to impose such discipline. In addition about one-fifth felt that the leadership style in the legislature is sufficiently flexible so that discipline becomes less important. Senators were more in agreement with the last statement than were assemblymen (see Table 3.6).

For about one-fourth of the respondents the roles played by the leadership were acceptable. A small percentage of members in both houses would like to have greater independence of the leadership and have the leadership consult more with members on legislative matters. There was, however, no universally perceived dissatisfaction

TABLE 3.6

Why Discipline Is Not Tight:
Legislators Who Believe Discipline Is Not Tight[a]

Why Is Discipline Not Tight?	Total (N = 36)	Assembly (N = 27) (in percent)	Senate (N = 9)
People Vote their Conscience (Individual Autonomy)	30	26	44
People Vote by Their District (Constituency)	17	19	11
Inability of Groups or Leaders to Impose Discipline	33	38	22
Flexible Leadership Style	22	19	33
There are Other Legislative Factions Than Just Party	11	15	—
Lack of Ideological Consensus	6	4	—

[a]Legislators gave multiple responses; therefore, columns do not total 100 percent.

Source: Compiled by the authors.

with the roles of the leaders and the way they were performing in those roles.

Partisanship and Policy-Making

New York's legislature is characterized by a long-established, vigorous, highly partisan competition. The Democrats, while usually the minority party, do occasionally capture one or both houses or the governorship. Democrats are still concentrated in the larger cities and a few smaller ones while Republican strength is still in the suburbs and rural areas. Under such conditions clear differences in party policies would be expected.[8] The differences, however, are more apparent than real and, as one Democratic leader notes, the Democrats in the legislature "go along" with a Republican governor when his program is considered to be in harmony with their own philosophy or their party has no alternative proposals.[9]

There are several reasons why partisanship has begun to be less pronounced. First, there is a wide spectrum of political ideologies in the legislature. Since the 1968 session the Democrats have harbored a reform group from New York City that has sought to reduce party control and develop a greater aura of state-wide concern.

Second, upstate Democrats, who are being elected in larger numbers in nominally Republican areas, more often resemble the Republicans they replace than they resemble downstate Democrats. On the Republican side it has already been noted that 11 assemblymen were elected to the 1969 legislature with substantial Conservative party help. Coupled with legislators from traditionally conservative Republican areas, they form a distinct ideological bloc.

Third, the rural-suburban-urban split in the legislature lessens partisanship. The concerns of legislators from suburban areas are similar and similar solutions are sought. The same is true of urban legislators, although legislators from small cities find more in common with each other than they do with large-city representatives. More and more, legislators from rural areas find themselves standing alone unless they can ally with representatives from smaller upstate suburban areas. New York City is a separate matter. The 94 legislators from this metropolis form a distinct group and at times vote as a bloc.* The dozen Republicans in the delegation often share the

---

*Democratic Minority Leader Stanley Steingut, referring to New York City Mayor John Lindsay's appeal for state aid in 1969, remarked that the City's legislators would "be constructive and help

viewpoints of their Democratic colleagues when it comes to legislation concerning New York City. The similarity of big-city problems has also drawn the legislators of the state's large cities closer together, blurring party lines. When the schools in New York City were decentralized in the 1969 legislative session, other city delegations gave the bills careful scrutiny, viewing each proposal as a prototype that might soon be extended to include their city's school districts.

Finally, there are the distinct interests of legislators—ideas and policy proposals that individual members take up as causes. To some extent each legislator becomes a lobbyist for that which he believes should be done. Legislators' interests often transcend the interests of district and might or might not have any coherent, powerful constituency or lobby behind them. A recent example in New York has been state financial aid to parochial schools and colleges, for several years an objective of Senate Majority Leader Brydges. To obtain a policy of minimum school aid in 1970 he released the majority members to "vote their consciences" on a liberal abortion bill, a bill he had hitherto opposed. Both bills were passed.

The lessening of political partisanship and the rise of other forms of partisanship have already been alluded to in legislators' responses to the survey. As noted in Table 3.6, 11 percent of the respondents who felt that party discipline was not tight indicated that there are legislative factions other than party. When legislators were asked if they felt that there are circumstances in which a member should not vote with his party, 59 percent said that this might happen if a measure conflicts with the interests of his district. Another cause of defection from party for 55 percent was an occasion on which dictates of conscience require them to vote differently (see Table 3.7). In fact, over one-half of those responding said that dictates of conscience would override the desires of the district's voters (see Table 3.8).

These findings demonstrate that the New York State legislature is a highly controlled and disciplined policy-making body. The leaders in both houses have used their appointment powers and their chairmanship of the rules committees to control the policy-making process to produce outcomes favorable to the majority party. Since 1968 there has been some slight loosening of the reins due to changes in leadership style and some lessening of political partisanship among the members. The ability of the leaders to manipulate the process, however, is still unimpaired. Against this background the behavior

---

solve the City's problems. There will be no politics here." Interview on WNED-TV, January 14, 1969.

TABLE 3.7

Circumstances when Legislator Does Not Vote with Party[a]

Circumstances when Legislator Does Not Vote with Party	Total (N = 104)	Assembly (N = 79) (in percent)	Senate (N = 25)
Never or Infrequently	3	1	8
Dictates of the Conscience	55	44	52
Conflicts with District Interests	59	61	52
Not a Party Bill	16	16	16
Your Vote Is Not Needed or It Is Released	2	—	8
Other	11	13	4

[a]Legislators gave multiple responses; therefore, columns do not total 100 percent.

Source: Compiled by the authors.

TABLE 3.8

Specific Considerations Given to Constituent Attitudes

Consideration Given to Attitudes of Constituents Before Voting	Total (N = 59)	Assembly (N = 42) (in percent)	Senate (N = 17)
Depends on Whether it is a State-wide Issue	5	7	—
Depends on the Issue Itself	27	26	29
"If My Conscience Dictates Otherwise" and/or "I know Better"	54	50	65
Other	14	17	6
	100	100	100

Source: Compiled by the authors.

of the legislature in educational policy-making will be presented next.

THE LEGISLATURE AND EDUCATIONAL POLICY-MAKING

Thus far the legislature has been considered in terms of party and leadership as proposed policy is moved into legislation. The focus now turns to the behavior of the legislature as it relates to educational policy-making. How much do legislators <u>know</u> about educational issues? Do they treat this policy-making area in a way different from the way they treat other substantive areas? What information is available to them? Which groups—internal and external—influence their deliberations? The remainder of this chapter summarizes the results of the survey and other study findings regarding these questions.

Level of Concern and Knowledge

Both Majority Leader Brydges and Speaker Duryea have exhibited continuing support for education. Brydges has long championed aid to private education and support for special education, helping to make New York a leader among the states in these fields. Duryea has shown concern for educational finance in general and aid to suburban schools in particular, helping to pass critical legislation in these areas.* In short, both of these men have provided progressive leadership in support of the needs of education in the state.

There is some evidence that these leaders' concerns and knowledge about education is shared by other members of the legislature. Results of the survey indicate that legislators are highly sensitive to educational issues. In fact, education was the policy area of special interest most frequently noted by responding legislators. Thirty-eight of the 117 respondents noted education as one of their areas of legislative expertise. The second most often noted area of legislative expertise, local government, ran far behind education, with 14 legislators checking this area as one in which they were experts. This declared interest in educational issues was confirmed by perceptions of legislators concerning the most critical issues before the legislature during the 1969 session. These issues,

---

*One educational interest group leader interviewed believes that Duryea "has used this education stance to propel himself into the speakership."

46

TABLE 3.9

Areas of Educational Expertise[a]

Area of Education in Which Legislator Feels Knowledgeable	Total (N = 38)	Assembly (N = 28) (in percents)	Senate (N = 10)
State Aid (Finance)	23	28	10
Programs for the Disadvantaged (i.e., SEEK)	20	24	10
Primary-Secondary Education	14	12	20
Higher Education	14	8	30
School Decentralization	9	12	—
Special Education	6	8	—
Elementary Education	6	8	—
Architectural Design	6	4	10
Secondary Education	3	—	10
N.Y.C. Problems	3	—	10
Regents Scholarships	3	4	—
All Areas	6	8	—
Other	11	8	20

[a]Legislators gave multiple responses; therefore, columns do not total 100 percent.

Source: Compiled by the authors.

as respondents saw them, were budgetary considerations (76 percent), decentralization of school districts (56 percent), and matters of public employment—in particular the state's collective negotiations law (23 percent). Thus the three most important issues before the legislature, according to respondents, all embraced education or education-related matters.

The 38 legislators who described themselves as experts in education exhibited a variety of specific interests in this policy area. Only 6 percent viewed themselves as experts in all educational areas. Further, only 23 percent of the respondents noted that finance is their major concern. These responses indicate that legislators have taken the time to become knowledgeable about substantive, or programmatic, as well as fiscal issues in education. As noted in Table 3.9, respondents were able to isolate 10 substantive interest areas ranging from programs for the disadvantaged to particular levels of education and school building design.

A final point related to legislators' concern with and knowledge of education should be made. The New York State legislature has established a mechanism to pursue long-range policy study and overcome possible legislative intransigence or deadlock—the Joint Legislative Committee (JLC). JLCs are formed by resolution of both legislative chambers and are made up of members appointed by the speaker and the majority leader. The JLC to Revise and Simplify the Education Law came into being in 1963. For the first several years it focused on recodifying the education law. In 1967 it turned its full attention to state aid for education, looking at the various sectors in the formula.

The power of the JLC in the late 1960s rested with the prestige and influence to its chairman, Clinton Dominick, a senior Republican senator who was also chairman of the Senate Education Committee.* He was looked on as an expert in the area of education by fellow legislators, by advisors to the governor, and by officials in the State Education Department. The majority leader in the senate usually supported his proposals and gave him a free hand with the committee. Other committee members represented critical areas, such as heavily populated, suburban Long Island and upstate rural areas.

In 1969 the JLC developed proposals for improved state aid that conflicted directly with the governor's desire to cut state spending. The governor prevailed and the chairman of the committee was placed in the uncomfortable position of leading the floor debate in favor of the governor's proposed changes in state aid. The following year the JLC was disbanded and the State Commission on Cost and Quality of Elementary and Secondary Education came into being.**

---

*Dominick was defeated in the primaries in 1970 apparently because of his pro-abortion stand.

**This state commission is often referred to as the Fleischmann Commission, after its chairman, Manly Fleischmann, a Buffalo lawyer. It is the latest in a series of state commissions called for by the governor's office. New York seems to establish a commission on education about every 10 years. The Fleischmann Commission, the first commission to make a comprehensive study of education since the Board of Regents' report of 1938, has proposed some gradual shifts in the structure of education as well as some basic changes in its financing and accountability. Regionalization, developed around the boards of cooperative educational services (the intermediate school government level) of which there were 56 in 1971, is recommended. The commission proposes total state financing education, with local property taxes for education being collected by the state and sent back to school districts on a per-pupil basis. The school

Educational Policy-Making: Is It Unique?

Does the legislature treat educational policy matters in the same manner that it treats other policy matters? This question can be examined on two levels: perceptions and actual behaviors exhibited by legislators concerning educational policy-making.

Legislators' Perceptions

At the perceptual level there is little difference in the processing of educational and other policies (see Table 3.10). For example, four

TABLE 3.10

Processing Legislation:
Education and Other Substantive Policy Areas

Question		Total (N = 107)	Assembly (N = 82) (in percent)	Senate (N = 26)
Are party conditions (e.g., considering position of party leaders and voting with party) the same when dealing with education as when dealing with other legislative areas?	Yes	78	78	76
	No	22	22	24
	Don't know	0	0	0
Do the leaders' activities differ in bills dealing with education?	Yes	23	24	19
	No	68	66	73
	Don't know	9	10	8
Does the JLC on education differ from other JLCs?	Yes	20	17	28
	No	56	59	48
	Don't know	24	24	24

Source: Compiled by the authors.

building level would be the unit of accountability and the principal would be the educator on the spot. How well these proposals will fare in the legislature remains to be seen. The first report was not released until January 1972. The legislature has not taken action on these recommendations as of this writing.

out of every five legislators responding to the survey felt that party conditions for voting are the same for education as they are for other substantive policy areas. To almost as great an extent respondents felt that legislative leaders behave in the same manner when processing educational policy as they do when processing policy in other areas. Finally, they felt that the JLC for education is similar in structure and function to other JLCs. As a caution, the "don't know" response, which is 9 percent for "the leaders' activities" and 24 percent for the JLC question, indicates that at least a minority of legislators are not fully clear about all of the intricacies involved in processing educational legislation.

More than 20 percent of those legislators responding, however, believed that the leaders' behavior regarding educational issues differs from their behavior regarding other legislative issues. When asked how this behavior differs, they gave the following answers:

Education Affects Everyone	24 percent
Education is Apolitical (nonpartisan)	18 "
More is Spent on Education than on Other Functions	19 "

Legislators who felt that the role of the party differs with regard to education responded in similar fashion:

Education is Apolitical (nonpartisan)	39 percent
Education Affects More People. It is a Very Important Issue	12 "
There is More Money Involved	9 "

When probed, these same respondents indicated that "apolitical" means that education is above party politics. They reasoned that because education affects everyone both parties benefit from adequate support for it. As they noted, however, the impact of education varies across the state. There are many differences, for example, in the level of property taxes and in the educational needs of public school children in school districts throughout the state. Legislators might have to take different positions on educational issues, therefore, depending upon the areas they represent. As a result party positions on educational issues in the legislature are often unrealistic.

Legislators' Behavior

The actual behavior of the legislature in processing legislation on education provides some assurance that the perception of the majority of responding legislators—that education is treated

50

much the same as other substantive policy areas—is accurate. A prime example is the way in which leaders assign educational bills to committees. The education committees in both chambers review many bills that are related to education* but bills that require budgetary appropriations are often withheld from these committees or closely supervised by the leadership. Those with budgetary considerations are all eventually sent to the Ways and Means Committee in the assembly and the Finance Committee in the senate where critical decisions are made to vote bills down, modify them, or report them out to the floor as recommended by the Education Committee. These fiscal committees, which can also deal a fatal blow to bills merely by refusing to act on them, are heavily dominated by the majority party in each chamber. This allows the speaker and the majority leader to maintain close control over bills that might affect the state's pending budget. As noted earlier, this same mode of operation is employed by the leadership in assigning and reviewing bills in other policy areas.

A second example is the role played by the party conference, planning sessions held by the Republicans and Democrats before key measures are brought to the floor for a vote. Often the parties require loyalty of members in the form of voting as dictated by the party conference. Breaking with the party on key conference vote decisions is rare among legislators.** When it does occur legislators guilty of disloyalty often suffer the consequences through removal from key positions, loss of patronage, or denial of key committee assignments.*** As with other policy areas when educational

---

*For example, "over 750 bills went before the Assembly Education Committee in the 1971 session of the legislature." State Education Department, Inside Education, January 1972, p. 7.

** In March 1968 Speaker Travia became the first legislative leader since 1865 to be embarrassed by a motion to bring a bill to the floor after he had asked his majority party in party conference to vote against the motion. The dissenting Democrats, all from upstate New York, risked party censure and loss of privileges in so doing. (New York Times, March 5, 1968, p. 1.)

***For example, in 1971 Assemblyman McFarland from the suburban Buffalo area was chairman of the assembly Republican Conference. In a key conference decision in December 1971 the party voted to support a tax increase proposed by the governor. McFarland decided to vote against the increase, ("My vote represented the views of the people in my district.") In a secret ballot vote his Republican assembly colleagues, by a reported two-to-one margin, removed him from his committee chairmanship. (Buffalo Evening News, January 29, 1972, p. A-6.)

measures affect the party's position either fiscally or ideologically, party members are "urged" to vote along party lines. This norm is often applied in education for such upcoming fiscal votes as proposed increases in the level of state aid for education. It might also be applied when nonfiscal but highly ideological votes are pending on such issues as collective negotiations for teachers or decentralization of New York City's schools.

In summary, both perceptual and behavioral evidence indicates that educational policy is processed in the same way that other policy matters are processed. Important considerations in education tend to be those that are also considerations in other policy areas. Thus New York City and upstate differences relate to labor-management and social welfare issues as well as to educational issues. Budgetary issues relate to highways and medical care as well as to education.

Internal Information Sources

If legislators are to understand the bills on which they are supposed to vote it is important that sufficient information be made available to them. There are three centralized sources of information available within the legislature, two that serve both houses and one that serves the assembly only. The oldest of these (1944) is the Legislative Bill Drafting Commission, composed of seven members. The commission provides technical advice, assistance, and research with respect to proposed legislation. Next in longevity is the Legislative Research Service, begun by Speaker Heck in 1947. The Research Service, with a staff of six people, is available to members of both houses to locate information on topics as requested. While the service is allegedly bipartisan, there are some indications that it has been operated largely for the benefit of the Republican members of the assembly.

The third source is the Assembly's Standing Committee Central Staff. Begun in 1969 as a part of Speaker Duryea's reforms, much of the staff's work has been devoted to the planning of "mini-sessions" held during the summer and fall months before the annual session begins. The purpose of these sessions is to bring standing committees into year-round operation and develop some continuity to legislative planning. In this respect, staff personnel assigned to committees (12 staff members, each responsible for three committees) develop background information on topics as requested by committee chairmen. Most of the data gathered are already extant and no program research is conducted for the committees. Thus far the purpose of the staff seems to be to supplement the information-gathering ability of committees through regularly assigned personnel and to provide their work with some continuity.

Other resources in the internal information system are the legislative staff members, counsels to the leaders, and counsels to majorities and—at times—minorities on committees. The nature of the work of these staff members is to present the leader or the committee chairmen (or the committee minority if it chooses to hire a counsel) with data on substantive issues. Counsels additionally explore questions of law and procedure. Many have long experience in the legislature and can also pass on their observations of the political context surrounding many topics. While the New York State legislature still has a number of part-time partronage positions on the legislative staff, there is a definite trend toward hiring expert help. There has been a decrease, moreover, in the number of lawyers and an increase in staff personnel specializing in such areas as government, economics, education, public administration, and systems analysis. Major committees such as Ways and Means in the assembly and the Finance Committee in the senate have full-time specialists in nearly all staff positions.

Counsels to the leaders in both houses play critical roles. For example, in 1969 the senate majority leader had eight counsels, each with responsibility in one or two major substantive areas. They advise the leader on the assignment of bills to committees and compare information developed by the committees with information of their own, advising the majority leader on alternatives. They also draft bills to put into operation the alternative decided upon by the leader or party conference.

In addition, specialized staff groups are put together by the leadership in each house. An example from the 1968 legislature will serve as an illustration. In the assembly Speaker Travia depended heavily on the staff put together by the secretary of the Ways and Means Committee to investigate alternatives to the governor's program. The secretary, a professor of political science on leave from Syracuse University, brought together a staff of approximately 12 full-time and part-time people. Most were young Ph.D. candidates in political science; several had some experience in government. This group developed program recommendations for Travia, examining alternatives to the state budget as presented by the governor. To obtain information the staff tapped various executive departments and municipal government agencies, but avoided the lobbyists and lobbying organizations because they felt such data would be inadequate. The staff also reviewed proposed legislation as assigned to it by the speaker, presenting recommendations for modification or endorsement as a part of the speaker's program.

Much of the Ways and Means Committee staff work was reviewed by what was informally known as the "Sunday Evening Group," which included the speaker, his counsel, the chairman of the Ways

53

and Means Committee, and the secretary of the committee staff. It was apparently in this group that choices were made among alternatives presented by the committee staff. The information supporting each alternative was shared within the staff and the immediate office of the speaker and parcelled out only when needed to reenforce positions taken.

A similar staff continued with Ways and Means when the Republicans gained a majority in 1969. Its use, however, has not been as extensive because the Republicans more readily accept the facts and figures of the governor's budget and usually obtain preferred treatment from executive agencies. Differences between the Republican majority in the legislature and the governor are often short-range and political rather than programmatic. That is, Republican legislators speak against the governor's budget largely because they do not feel that they can go home looking like spendthrifts.

There are, of course, external sources of information available to legislators. In education such information comes mainly from the Board of Regents, the State Education Department, and educational interest groups. More will be said about these sources later. For the present it should be noted that legislators indicated that internal sources of information are employed more extensively than are external. Seventy-four percent of responding legislators noted internal sources of information as a primary information base, whereas only 24 percent noted interest groups and 16 percent identified executive agencies as primary sources of information.

Influence Sources and Educational Policy-Making

Because they play central roles in the policy-making process legislators are targets of internal and external individuals and groups who, as actors in the policy process, attempt to influence their decisions. Within the legislature itself there are at least four sources of such influence. First, there is the legislative leadership, which controls the assignment and flow of bills and supervises the debate and voting on key bills when they reach the senate and assembly floors. Second, there are committees that can vote down or approve bills assigned to them and disseminate or withhold information that might influence legislators' positions on such measures. Third, there are legislators who have gained reputations as experts in such policy areas as education; their views are usually listened to with great interest by other legislators. Finally, there are staff members whose primary function is to study bills, develop content resumes, and offer suggestions for action to the leadership.

Legislators are influenced by four distinct groups that are in their environment and are themselves actors in the educational policy-making process. Most immediately they are influenced by the governor and his executive agencies. The governor presents the legislature with his budget at the outset of the legislative session. He also makes general and specific program recommendations at this time. Much of the legislature's time is spent debating, modifying, and voting on the governor's budget and program proposals. The governor also exerts influence through his position as the highest state-wide elected official, his relationship with party leaders in the legislature, his veto power, and such key executive officers as the governor's counsels, who often negotiate with legislators for the governor, and representatives of the Division of the Budget, who keep a close watch over the legislature's budget-related activities. Second, the Board of Regents and the State Education Department— the former based upon its acknowledged prestige and the latter based upon its research capacity and lobbying potential—can exert significant influence on the legislature. Third, educational interest groups and allied lay groups, using their formal organizations as well as "grass-roots" pressure can bring their influence to bear upon legislator's activities. Finally, and possibly most frequently considered, is the public, which can vote for or against legislators.

The influence bases of internal and external groups vary.* Those within the state government structure—the governor and the Board of Regents—can depend upon their authoritative positions to help them gain legislators' ears. Those outside the state government, like educational interest groups, must devise informal influencing strategies.

How effective are these internal and external groups in influencing the state legislature? In our survey legislators were asked to discriminate among these influence sources in terms of their impact on positions they take on pending educational legislation. Table 3.11 summarizes their responses to this question.

Legislators could differentiate between "important" and "very important" influence sources. According to responding legislators, experts in the legislature and the views of the people in their districts rank the highest as being "very important" in the formulation of their views on educational legislation. The concern of responding

_____

*To the sources of internal and external influence discussed in this section one could add the mass media, the federal government, other states, and the courts. They are not included here because they lack the degree of immediate and continuing influence that characterizes those described.

TABLE 3.11

Importance of Groups in Influencing
Legislators' Views about Educational
Legislation

| | Perceptions of Responding Legislators | | |
Groups	Very Important	Important (in percent)	Unimportant
Experts in the Legislature	55	43	2
People in the Districts	48	46	6
Education Committees	39	54	7
Educators Back Home	34	58	8
Educational Interest Groups	25	61	14
Legislative Staff Opinions	24	52	24
Committees Other than Education	14	52	34
Executive Department Agencies[a]	8	66	26
Party Leaders	6	56	38

[a]Because many legislators subsume the Board of Regents and the State Education Department under executive department agencies, legislators were asked to rank specifically these educational government bodies. Of those who ranked the executive department agencies as important or very important, 82 percent cited the Board of Regents and the State Education Department as the agencies exercising most specific influence on their views concerning education. This far outdistanced the second ranking agency, the Division of the Budget, which was noted by only 15 percent of the responding legislators as specifically influencing their views concerning education.

---

legislators with the way legislative experts in education feel and the views of their constituents is interesting. These are two distinct reference groups. The views of the first group are sought because of its knowledge, the views of the second because of its voting strength. One group that crosses over both of these appeals are educators back home (34 percent of the respondents noted them as "very important") who have a knowledge base and also can be very influential in supporting or not supporting legislators' continued candidacies for reelection.

The executive department agencies and the party leaders rank the lowest as being "very important" to views on educational legislation. The relatively low ranking of educational interest groups and the very low ranking of executive department agencies and party leaders are unexpected. One explanation might be that education, a locally oriented issue that might not require a party position on many bills, tends to differ from the party domination found in other policy areas.

* * *

The legislature, then, is the central locus of the policy process. Legislators, however, are but one of several groups that interact in the educational policy-making process. Others, as we have stressed, include the governor, the Board of Regents, the State Education Department, and educational interest groups. Legislators, if they hope to enact legislation that will be fully implemented are dependent upon their contribution to that process. Now that the perceptions and behavior of legislators have been depicted, it is necessary to move on to parallel discussions of these other actor groups. The first will be the governor and his executive staff because the relationship between the legislature and the governor is so direct and so great.

4

**THE GOVERNOR
AND HIS PROGRAM**

Few state governors have the combination of administrative and political weaponry to control both government and party that are at the disposal of the governor of New York State. The weapons that make the governorship a powerful executive and political office also make it a critical part of the legislative process. The governor of New York is, to use Claudius O. Johnson's term, the chief legislator of the state.[1] As the state's top elected official the governor has public visibility that makes him a paramount molder of public opinion about the state's well-being. In his annual message and budget he outlines a program for the growth and progress of the state. A range of veto powers, control of budget operations, and powers of appointment are the means by which the governor influences the movement of his program through the legislative process. Legislative leaders, particularly those of his own party, must come to grips with his proposals before they begin to examine alternatives.

This chapter will focus on the governor's legislative role, illuminating how his executive and political powers are an integral part of the policy-making process. Education as a policy area presents opportunities for variation because of a tradition of political noninterference in education and the fact that the Board of Regents is constitutionally responsible for education. Educational policy-making, particularly for state financing, however, is increasingly being approached by the governor in the same way he approaches other areas of state responsibility.

DEVELOPMENT OF THE GOVERNOR'S POWERS

The governor of New York is the program leader and chief legislator of the state. Legislative domination of state government, which had existed since colonial times, was ended in a period of government reform between 1920 and 1927. Under the leadership of Governor Alfred E. Smith, the executive branch was reorganized to make the governor truly the chief executive. State-wide elective offices were reduced from 19 to 4: governor, lieutenant governor, comptroller, and attorney general. Over 185 state agencies were consolidated into 19 departments, later expanded to 21, and the heads of each, except for audit, control, law, and education,* became appointees of the governor. An administrative cabinet system was established and department heads were made responsible to him.[2] The governor's term was extended from two to four years in 1934, giving him the advantage of a term twice as long as that of legislators.[3]

Reform also brought into being the executive budget, giving the governor responsibility for planning and executing the state's financial program. The governor was given the task of preparing and sending to the legislature a balanced budget detailing proposed expenditures and estimated revenues. Departmental requests for funding had to clear the governor's office for inclusion in the budget. The legislature might reduce the budget but could not increase it without providing tax legislation to bring in additional revenues. This meant that the legislature rather than the governor would bear the onus for increased taxes. Confronted by the governor's veto powers, including the line-item veto by which the governor could veto discrete appropriations, the legislature was forced to bargain with him on fiscal policy.

The consolidation of state departments and the appointive powers given to the governor placed a vast amount of patronage under his control. This not only reinforced the governor's ability to deal with the legislature but also increased his ability to control his own party in the state. Local party leaders could quickly be brought in line by the threat of a cutoff in state jobs. More than that, local political leaders could quickly be stripped of power by the governor's decision to dispense patronage through a "more dependable member" of the local organization.

The full meaning of these changes was not realized until the Great Depression ended. Beginning in 1943, in his first term, Governor Thomas E. Dewey, a Republican, set the pattern for others to follow. With Republican majorities in both houses of the legislature, he proceeded to outline sound, progressive programs for state

----

*The Board of Regents continued, as a constitutional body, to appoint the commissioner of education. (See Chapter 5.)

government. While his administrative cabinet advised him on the substance of programs, his "kitchen cabinet," composed of his counsel, the speaker of the assembly and the majority leader of the senate, advised him on the political aspects of seeing the program through. Dewey used patronage with ruthless effectiveness, not only to bring legislators in line, but to bring county organizations to heel behind his policies.[4] Dewey's control was so complete that only one major revolt was ever launched against him in the legislature in three terms. (It was not successful.) The pattern has been refined little since the Dewey administration and then only to the extent of putting a velvet glove on the iron fist.

PROGRAM AND POWER

The governor's power gives him tremendous leverage in the legislative process. The concentrated power of the governor pitted against the diffuse power of the legislature tends to tip the balance in favor of the executive. It might still be said that the governor proposes and the legislature disposes. But the governor's powers are more than sufficent to bring the legislature to dispose along lines he has laid down. How closely legislative results match executive proposals is conditioned by several factors, including the party affiliations of the governor and majorities in each house, the needs of New York City, and the thrust of the governor's program itself.

Party Affiliation

Party affiliations of the governor and the legislative majority are important because the leadership in each house has its own means of maintaining party discipline among members. Even a governor of the same party would find himself in difficulty if he attempted to undermine the prerogatives of the leadership in promoting his policies in the legislature. The governor must always consult with the legislative leadership.

The smoothest legislative operations in carrying out a governor's program have been those situations in which the same party holds the governorship and majorities in both houses. Republican governors have found it relatively easy to work with legislative leaders in keeping Republican majorities in line. Governor Dewey, for example, gave Speaker of the Assembly Oswald Heck a free hand in rewarding and punishing Republican assemblymen. Perry Duryea, speaker during the Rockefeller administration, has had the same leeway, even to the extent of bringing about the dismissal of the assembly's

Republican Conference chairman when he voted against an administration proposal for increased taxation in a 1971 special session. Nor are the leaders themselves immune to the governor's power. In 1966 Rockefeller saw to it that George Ingalls, then Republican minority leader of the assembly, was removed in favor of Perry Duryea because Ingalls did not seem sufficiently enthusiastic about the governor's program. It is difficult to say how well a Democratic governor would fare with a Democratic legislature. This has not occurred since 1935 and, given the splits and factions within New York State Democracy, it is difficult to predict what would occur.

With a governor of one party and a legislative majority of the other, however, it has been demonstrated that the governor can still be quite effective. Rockefeller faced this situation in 1965-66 and managed through judicious compromises with Democratic legislative leaders generally to continue the thrust of his programs. A major factor in this situation was the realization of Speaker Anthony Travia that a record of nonconstructive opposition to governor would further reduce the slim chance of retaining Democratic control in succeeding elections. Rockefeller saw to it that sufficient patronage was available to Democrats and that certain proposals of the Democratic majority were incorporated into his own program to assure assembly passage. He was also willing to use his influence over Republican legislators in both houses to assure passage of compromise measures.

On the other hand, a Democratic governor facing a Republican-controlled legislature in recent times has not had nearly as much success. The administration of W. Averell Harriman (1955-58) was unable to bring the Democratic minority in both houses firmly into line behind the governor's proposals, which were designed to enlist the aid of Republican lawmakers in their passage. The majority then proceeded to put through its own legislation, modifying it only to the extent necessary to avoid Harriman's vetos.

Needs of New York City

The needs of New York City are another crucial factor with which the governor must come to grips. The 96 legislators from the five boroughs have shown some tendency to vote as a bloc, almost regardless of party affiliation, on matters that affect the welfare of the City in general and their own reelection in particular. Any governor's proposals that seem to mitigate against the interests of the City or favor upstate areas over the metropolis, particularly measures dealing with housing, transportation, and, above all, financial aid to city government, can be expected to receive close scrutiny from the City delegation. A Republican gubernatorial

candidate has an additional problem. He must do well in New York
City if he expects to win the election. A preponderant Democratic
majority in the five boroughs cannot be offset by suburban and rural
Republican areas upstate. Thus, a Republican governor who expects
to be reelected needs to make his record palatable to New York
City voters.

The Governor's Program

The final factor is the nature of the program itself. In the past
30 years New York has been fortunate in that its governors have,
by and large, put forth sound programs designed to meet the needs of
the state. While these programs have not been all that each interest
group wanted, they have been programs that, taken as a whole, provided more than just something for everyone. Reflecting the entire
gamut of state responsibilities and concerns, the governor's program is drawn from many sources. The requests of the various
state agencies form its base. Consideration is given to the findings
of joint legislative committees or special state commissions, as well
as proposals from other governments, especially those of cities.
The governor's program also attempts to reflect the perceived concerns of the citizens. New York's Clean Waters Program, for example,
came into being in 1970 as a result of public demand for cleaning up
the environment. Following the prison riot at Attica in 1971,
Rockefeller's program reflected a call for prison reform through a
sizable increase in the funds requested for the Corrections Department.
   While there is a degree of internal lobbying by state agencies,
the final filter for all program inputs is the staff in the executive
department, both within the immediate office of the governor and
in several executive agencies, Their task is to review all requests
and recommendations from all sources for their fiscal, legal, and
political implications. The staff balances these requests against the
governor's platform and other statements to make a set of final
recommendations on the program.
   In the next section the factors of party affiliation, New York
City's needs, and program development will be examined for their
effect on educational policy-making. The governor's relationships
with the Board of Regents will also be more fully explored.

THE GOVERNOR AND EDUCATION

All state governors must deal with education as a state responsibility. While there are few political gains to be made for the

governor and his party by promoting continued expansion and improvement in education, neglect of education carries a potential for political embarrassment and some loss of support in the legislature. As Nicholas A. Masters has pointed out, there is the central question of state-versus-local financial support: What can be allocated to education within the total financial program of the state? Will there be sufficient relief for local school tax burdens?[5] There are severe pressures on governors to see that education obtains its "fair share." Not only do state education agencies, the internal lobby for education, and professional and lay groups concerned with education in the state— the external lobby press governors on this point. Governors also receive pressure from legislators from districts in which school financial problems are thought to be serious.

Beyond questions of finance, it falls to the governor to establish a climate for consideration of educational needs by demonstrating his personal interest in education.[6] If a governor projects his public image, and at times his party's image, in a positive stance toward education, he can enhance the chances for continued progress in education. On the other hand, a governor's opposition to policy changes in education can spell legislative trouble for his other proposals. There are variations in the several states, as both Masters and Stephen K. Bailey have pointed out. While the ability to establish a climate is related to the power of the governor in the policy process, other elements are the relative strength of the state board of education and the history of citizens' expectation's for government action in the field of education.

In New York State the record of gubernatorial involvement in the expansion and development of education is long and illustrious. Governor Theodore Roosevelt was a prime mover in the 1904 act that brought about the unification of educational policy-making under the Board of Regents. In the 1920s Alfred E. Smith set the basic pattern for state aid to public schools. Herbert H. Lehman saw to it that formula aid was paid to schools even in the midst of the Great Depression. Thomas E. Dewey established the State University system and approved the foundation principle, developed by Columbia University's Paul Mort, for support of public education. Nelson Rockefeller expanded the University system and established the shared-cost principle as the basis of state aid to elementary and secondary schools. Over the years state commissions have helped and advised the governor on costs and quality of schools, school building programs, and teachers' salaries. The result has been the development of a tradition of gubernatorial support of education as a state responsibility.

At the same time the Board of Regents, as a policy body for education, has not been overshadowed by gubernatorial actions.

While every governor has felt free to ignore the board's recommendations when they clashed with his own programs, the board still plays a significant role in shaping education, through both advising the governor and bringing educational problems to public view. Governors have also been able to diminish the role of party politics in most educational questions by adopting the regents' recommendations. The regents thus have served to maintain the image of keeping education out of politics.

In New York State there is an expectation that public education will be given an appropriate place in state programs. People have come to expect the governor and the legislature to use their authority to provide adequately for it. There is also some expectation, as James B. Conant points out, that educational policy-making will not become a political football.[7]

The Strategy for Education

The main concern in policy-making for elementary and secondary education is finance. In this area the governor reviews the requests of the regents and then carefully delineates the policies believed to be feasible for incorporation in the budget. In other areas concerning the field of education the governor tends to rely on Board of Regents to present proposals with which he can live politically. If new appropriations are not involved and if, on the basis of available information, their proposals will not cause political problems, the governor usually leaves the regents to work them out with the legislature.

Aid amounts for local schools, the major items in the Board of Regents' annual legislative request, are determined by previously enacted formulas, but the funds must be included in the governor's budget. Increases in the proportion of the state share or changes in the formulas as well as new programs, such as special aids to city schools, require new legislation and further appropriations. These requests have to be considered within the total spending plan that the governor sends to the legislature.

The budget, carefully tailored to political and economic conditions, is the fiscal expression of the governor's program. His objective is to get the budget through the legislature intact. When he reduces aid to education or fails to include increases and changes that educators consider essential, he can expect to face a legislature that is being pressed by educators and their friends to modify the budget. Those modifications might include reducing some other portion of the budget to raise the share for education.

On other politically sensitive proposals regarding education, such as decentralization of city systems, racial integration, public employee negotiations, and intergovernmental relations, the governor gives consideration largely in terms of the impact they will have in the various jurisdictions, the towns and cities. The political impact these proposals will have on various legislative delegations is also taken into account.

Proposals regarding curriculum, teacher certification, and similar "nonpolitical" issues are usually considered as totally within the Board of Regents' province. The governor rarely touches on these items in his program and he usually does not even offer an opinion unless remaining silent would be politically embarrassing.

There are obvious advantages in the form of minimum political risk for the governor in this strategy. When the regents' financial requests coincide with his own the governor can use their pronouncements to buttress his position with the legislature. When they are excessive the governor can reduce their requests and point to his achievement in economizing, relying on the legislature to shy away from adding new taxes to pay for education.

In other education matters, the governor has a choice of leaving the Board of Regents to its own devices for policy change or stepping in with an endorsement and political help in the legislature. If a proposal of regents fails in the legislature it is not the governor's proposal that has failed. If the regents succeed the governor can bask in the reflected light, taking credit for a change that came about under his administration.

The governor must be ready to compromise when a sufficient number of legislators find it unpalatable to go home without doing more for education than the governor has proposed. This kind of leverage affects other parts of his program even if it does not earn him a label as one unfriendly to education. He might have to give a bit more to education if he wants, say, changes in social welfare, in the prison system or in the regulation of business. How well a governor can weather these situations is a test of his political skill.

The Governor's Program for Education

Within the state government, beyond the Board of Regents and its staff, the State Education Department, major inputs to the governor's program for education come from the Division of the Budget (DOB), the Office of Planning Coordination, and the governor's staff headed by the secretary to the governor and his counsels. This Chapter will detail the input and activities of the three executive department information arms, leaving an in-depth examination of Board of Regents to the next.

Division of the Budget

The Division of the Budget (DOB) dates from the first Dewey administration. In brief, it is the governor's program arm, the agency that researches the balance sheets of existing programs and the potential cost of proposed programs. The DOB is respected for its thoroughness and the high quality of its work. Legislative counsels and legislators themselves often turn to it for needed information about state fiscal matters.

The director of the DOB from 1959-70 was T. Norman Hurd, a former university professor, member of the Board of Regents, and appointee of Governor Rockefeller.* One objective of Hurd's directorship was to improve the planning and evaluating capability of the division. He initiated a planning, program and budget system in 1967 to provide better control of programs, elimination of overlap in state agencies' activities, and development of comparative data for budgetary decisions. Operational problems in both the agencies and the division, however, have brought about the substitution of a less detailed method—program analysis review.

The division's most important task is the development of the governor's budget. This document is hammered out before the legislature convenes in January. It contains budgetary requests from all state departments for the coming fiscal year, including proposed new programs. There are also economic forecasts of the state's ability to meet these obligations, including a detailed breakdown of taxation and other revenue sources, including federal aids.

In putting the budget together the DOB gathers data about program needs and department activities. The division's staff works closely with the agencies to help them develop forecasts of their needs and holds hearings at which the agencies defend their proposed budgets. Once it has this information, the DOB staff brings the requests into line with expected gubernatorial preferences, both fiscal and political. Through this long and detailed process the executive budget takes form.

In dealing with the area of elementary and secondary education the division finds itself in a heightened political situation. Because of the relative independence of the Board of Regents as a separate control board, its staff, the State Education Department, feels less pressure than other state agencies to adhere to division guidelines

---

*Hurd has since been appointed to the newly created post of director of state operations and is responsible for both budgetary and planning activities in the executive department.

and deadlines in submitting its budget. Often the department does not obtain the Board of Regents' approval of the program until several months after the division's deadline. Further, when the regents' proposals are transmitted to the division there has been a simultaneous release of the regent's legislative program for public reading. The division finds thus itself wrestling with requests that are already public knowledge. If the division's staff begins earlier, it finds itself with insufficient information concerning educational needs. When this happens the staff occasionally takes the initiative in developing education requests for the governor's approval, according to a division staff member. This puts the division in the position of initiating education programs, thus in conflict with the State Education Department.

A second political problem in education is the balance between state and local funding. The division is responsible for making the first estimate of this problem. A decrease in state aid that forced increases in local taxes could lead to political repercussions. At the same time increases requested by the regents could lead to requests for new taxes at the state level. Special aid for rapidly growing school districts or urban aid means the favoring of certain districts over others. The political ramifications of these factors are taken into consideration by the division in reaching funding requests that the governor can live with politically in facing both the public and the legislature.

The Division of the Budget provides carefully acquired technical information and is alert to the political implications of alternative actions with regard to education. Political decisions are made by the governor's immediate staff, but it is the DOB that embodies those decisions in the state's fiscal plan.

Office of Planning Coordination

The Office of Planning Coordination (OPC) was created in 1967.* Its director until 1970, Charles Lanigan, was a Rockefeller appointee.** Rockefeller established the agency to obtain information for making decisions based on economic, social, and political goals for the state. Staffed by highly trained and skilled economists and other behavioral

---

*In 1971 the OPC was consolidated with several other quasi-planning agencies and became the Office of Planning Services. It reports to the director of state operations.

**Lanigan resigned to become Republican state chairman.

scientists, the OPC attempts to get the several government departments to clarify their goals and objectives and to coordinate the planning of programs to reach those goals. Broad goals have been identified but not well delineated.

As the departments develop their programs, looking forward to budget presentation, the OPC reviews their objectives to see that they harmonize with state goals. Proposed programs of the several agencies are also examined for their appropriateness in terms of resources and for points at which joint or interdepartmental activity might be desirable.

The Board of Regents' responsibility for education lodges the functional responsibility for educational planning almost totally within the State Education Department. Thus, according to an OPC official, the principal role of the OPC is to review department proposals in budget development. This consists essentially of checking the department's proposals against objectives that have been set by the regents. The OPC also checks on federal funding for education because it is responsible for coordinating all state-federal-local planning in New York.

The changes in planning arrangements, made in 1971, have reduced and retarded the scope of the planning agency's activities. There is now less concern with over-all state goals and greater emphasis on the coordination of objectives as developed by the functional departments. The planning agency thus has the role of examining and coordinating objectives, while the Division of the Budget moves to take a more critical look at programs as well as their financing.

The Governor's Program Staff

The governor's program staff is concerned with the basic political decisions that shape the governor's program. Staff members are designated as counsel, assistant counsels, and program associates, all coordinated through a close aide, the secretary to the governor. They function as advisors, listening posts, conveyers of messages, trouble shooters and case workers. Their areas of operation are loosely defined. For example, an assistant counsel might have regular duties with regard to legislation concerning two or three departments, such as Education, Mental Hygiene, and Conservation, but might also be responsible for a functional area broadly labeled "education." In following this functional route, he might occasionally be involved with many departments. While there is a good deal of overlap in broadly delineated functional areas, there are two main divisions of labor: programs and operations monitored by the program associates reporting to the secretary to the governor and policy and legal aspects monitored by the governor's counsels and assistant counsels. Both result in advice to the governor on the political ramifications of his program.[8]

The secretary to the governor and the governor's counsel are also in contact with various elements of the governor's party, receive representations from other governments including those of towns and cities, and listen to the concerns of organized interest groups. Formal position papers as such are rarely developed, but there is a constant stream of memoranda to the governor advising him of difficulties in current programs, dissatisfactions among citizens and party members, or suggestions for future modifications in programs.

The counsel's office provides more comprehensive information about bills originating in the legislature that bear on the governor's program. They develop "bill jackets," which contain data and information from groups and individuals concerned with a measure. If the bill is passed the governor has 10 days in which to veto the measure or it becomes law without his signature. Five of these days are used by the counsel to complete the bill jacket through soliciting organizations and persons who would be concerned but who have not yet given an opinion. Once the information is collected, the counsel drafts a 5- to 10-page opinion summarizing the views pro and con, developing legal ramifications, and finally making a recommendation for action by the governor.

Within the governor's staff education is viewed with ambivalence. Members find the scope of the regents' responsibilities overwhelming and difficult to grasp. The counsels, however, have developed a close relationship with the Law Division of the Education Department. They feel they can rely on the division to help them solve legal problems and define the policy implications of proposed legislation. The program associates have no such help. Their contact person has been the deputy commissioner of education, the person in charge of initial program development for the department. While cooperation has been good, the program associates complain that hard information is difficult to obtain and that there are intolerable delays in getting at what information is available.[9]

Executive-Legislative Relations

Once the legislative session begins education receives about the same attention from the governor and his staff as any other policy area in his program. The Division of the Budget and the Office of Planning Coordination fill requests for information made by legislators and committees. The governor's counsels explain his proposals to the counsels of the legislative leaders and committees. As counterproposals appear the staff carefully compares them with the governor's program, occasionally suggesting their incorporation but more often pointing out how they fail to meet the governor's goals. At times they solicit agency opinions on other proposals or request agency help in exposing undesirable bills. In the Rockefeller administration, these tasks have been well coordinated so that both the governor and the legislative leadership are kept informed.

During the session there is close continuing contact between the governor and the legislative leaders of his party. Rockefeller relies on his counsel and secretary to carry messages. These two men also help by contacting recalcitrant legislators and presenting the governor's point of view. These are also the men who reach beyond legislators to their county leaders if the need arises. By and large, however, Rockefeller has let legislative leaders develop their own strategy in working with the rank and file of the legislature. When crises arise the governor is available and consults with the leaders to find solutions.

When help from the minority party is needed, the governor meets with its leaders if the matter cannot be ironed out through legislative cooperation. If an agency program request is to be cut as part of the solution, the secretary to the governor relays the news to the agency head and obtains the agency's reaction.

All compromise decisions about the budget or other program measures are ultimately made by the governor. The same is true of bills that can cause potential political difficulties for the governor or his party. The chief executive relies on his advisors and the legislative leaders of his party for their suggestions but he makes the final choices among alternatives.

* * *

In developing his program the governor is mindful of party affiliation in the legislature, the special needs of New York City, and a balance of fiscal, social, and political considerations. He relies on his staff to provide information and advice that will result in a set of proposals that meet the objectives of his administration and, at the same time, draw sufficient support to meet opposition.

In education the governor also considers the proposals of the Board of Regents in drawing up his program. The central concern is finance and its place in the budget. The governor's strategy for education is designed to minimize political risk to his image and to the passage of his program vis à vis education. If the regents' program agrees with his, the governor's position is reinforced. If there is disagreement, the governor may leave it up to the legislature to wrestle with the Regents' requests. The nature of the Board of Regents' proposals and their development will be examined in the next chapter.

5

THE REGENTS

The Board of Regents of the University of the State of New York is unique among state boards responsible for education. No other state board has the legislative, executive, and judicial powers granted the regents either in constitution or in statutes. Nor does any other board have the august prestige of this body, which has been in continuous existence since 1784. In the past the board has molded public and government opinion on education by virtue of its place atop the state's education pyramid and an image of being above politics in its approach to educational problems. Since the late 1950s, however, the regents have been drawn more and more into the political arena by the changing nature of school problems. The response of the board has been to fashion its own political instruments for seeking policy change in education.

This chapter will examine the emerging role of the regents in the policy process. It will review the powers of the board, the steps in program development, and the activities the board pursues in getting its proposals into the policy-making process.

THE REGENTS' REALM

The Board of Regents is the public policy board for all educational activities in the state, both public and private. As a policy body it is responsible for planning the board educational program of the state, chartering schools and colleges, regulating licensing in medicine and health-related professions, public accounting, and teaching (the one major exception is law), and supervising public and nonpublic schools, adult education, and special education. The board is the coordinating agency for higher education and sets the standards for college and university degree programs. The regents also have authority over museums and libraries and chartering educational television stations. In addition to these legislative and administrative powers the board has judicial authority to censure professional misconduct and revoke the charters of institutions that fail to meet its standards. The board also validates the judicial decisions of the commissioner of education, who has final authority in public school matters such as disputes over district boundaries, actions by local boards, student discipline, and teacher dismissals that might be brought before him on appeal.[1] These independent powers are of such scope that Stephen K. Bailey questioned their consonance with American constitutional principles of separation of powers and checks and balances.[2] Yet the Board of Regents has continued with little diminution of its powers for nearly 200 years.

A Fourth Branch of Government

The board is sometimes referred to as the fourth branch of state government. Its separate powers to regulate education as well as its independence of the executive branch, of which it is an organizational part, have contributed to this image. Moreover, the structure of the board and its staff arm, the State Education Department, reinforce the idea.

The board is made up of 15 members elected by joint ballot of the legislature, one from each of the state's 11 judicial districts and four at-large.* The term of office is 15 years, one member's term expiring each year. By custom the major religious and ethnic groups of the state are recognized among the membership. The first woman regent was elected in 1927. The first recognition of blacks came in 1966.

Historically the board has been dominated by men and women of sound Republican background, reflecting that party's domination of the legislature and the unofficial recommendations of Republican governors. In recent years, however, a more bipartisan approach has prevailed, aided by two years of Democratic control of the legislature.

The State Education Department is the staff of the regents. The board appoints the commissioner of education to serve "at its pleasure" as the chief administrative officer of the department. He is one of the three executive agency heads not appointed by the

---

*New York is one of 11 states in which the state board is elected by vote of the people or the peoples' representatives.

governor. Chosen for his professional competence in education, the commissioner executes the regents' policies and advises the board on matters under its jurisdiction. The commissioner represents the board with the governor, the legislature, the schools, and the public. A number of these tasks are delegated to his associate commissioners and to his several executive assistants. The department hierarchy in 1969 consisted of a deputy commissioner, 5 associate commissioners, 15 assistant commissioners, 30 division directors and 55 bureau heads.

There are some 3,000 employees in the department. Over 1,000 are classified as professionals and administer the myriad of activities that are the responsibility of the regents. In sheer enormity the administrative task is greater than that of any other state agency. The department oversees 4,000 public schools, 2,000 nonpublic schools, 230 colleges and universities, as well as 1,000 libraries and museums.[3] In addition to this supervision department personnel evaluate and record information about programs, expenditures, enrollments, and other facets of educational operations. It is on this information that department requests for finance and other policy proposals are based.

The estimated expenditures of the department totaled $2.2 billion in 1969 of which $1.9 billion went to public school operating aid, another $29.7 million to special aids, $52.0 million to urban aid, and $1.5 million to the administrative functions of the department. In 1971 the budget totaled $2.6 billion, continuing the 20-plus percent rate of increase of the past decade. Planned expenditures for elementary and secondary education accounted for nearly 28 percent of the state budget in 1971-72.[4]

The Regents in the Policy Process

The regents' role in the policy process can be understood only in terms of its historic role and the shift that the board seems to be making toward a new role. The apolitical image of the regents and their great prestige as a lay board of distinguished citizens have become less than effective as influences for promoting the regents' proposals. As issues in education have come to involve larger social and political questions such as racial integration, the rights of public employees, redistricting, and increasing taxation, the board has been drawn more and more into the political arena. Thus the board has begun to gauge its actions more in terms of political viability and acceptance.

The thrust of the board is to develop state-wide goals for education, particularly for public schools, and to determine what is needed to achieve those goals. In the past the board carefully enunciated its policies with some balance between the proper advancement of the schools and the climate of public opinion. The scales have been tipped slightly to the conservative side with the board tending to avoid radically new proposals. The governor and the legislature were expected to provide the necessary funds regardless of their opinions about the policy.[5] If new legislation was needed, that, too, was expected to be enacted without much questioning of department officials when they met with legislative committees. Once policy has been made the department has been directed to carry it out.

When controversy arose the board and the State Education Department sought to handle it totally within the educational government. The regulatory and judicial powers of the regents were used to correct the situation by changing the rules without reference to the views of the legislature or of the governor. Conant's depiction of New York's solution to the teacher preparation and certification controversy arising out of the sputnik crisis in 1957 is an excellent example. The department set up committees to study the situation and gathered opinions from the public as well as from teachers and other interested parties. The regulations for certification were redrawn and promulgated by the regents.[6] It was also probably the last major issue to be settled totally within the educational government.

With the new emphasis on the educationally disadvantaged, demands for increased accountability as school budgets increase, and a greater public understanding of education as a pervasive social question, the regents have been drawn toward a more open, political participation in the policy-making process. This is evidenced in the stepped-up research effort in the State Education Department and the development of an annual legislative program by the regents.

Studies of educational problems have been made by the regents in the past. The landmark Regents Inquiry into the Character and Cost of Public Education in New York State[7] in 1936-38 was not paralleled in scope and depth until the State Commission on Quality, Cost, and Financing began its work in 1970. Studies of more limited focus have been conducted by divisions of the department in increasing numbers since 1965. Findings have resulted in the publication of position papers on major topics such as the urban school crisis, reading improvement, and preschool education. About a dozen papers were issued through 1972. Many of the ideas embodied in these documents have found their way into the regents' annual recommendations for legislative action.

The regents began to issue an annual legislative program in 1962. Each year advocates the major changes in state policy for education that the board believes are needed to meet the broad goals it has set for education in the state. These include assessment of the fiscal needs of the schools, requests for funding necessary to begin new programs, suggested enabling legislation for extending educational opportunity, and modifications of the law to permit participation in federal programs. In 1968 it contained an unprecedented endorsement of a tax increase to provide added school aid requested by the regents.[8]

The release of the program is made in November or December just before the legislature convenes. Addressed to the legislature and the governor, copies are also distributed to major educational groups in the state, school officials, and the mass media. Each legislator receives a copy as do members of the governor's staff.

Program Development

The regents' legislative program is developed within the education department and adopted by the board with the advice of the commissioner. The process of program development might be pictured in terms of a funnel. At the larger end proposals from sources both within and without the department are sifted by the department's hierarchy. Proposals that reflect the board's goals and current policies or are a logical extension of them are sent to appropriate department units for review. The result is a series of reports recommending inclusion or exclusion of each idea as well as data to support the recommendation. At the same time the department's law division examines the legal feasibility of each proposal. In this screening much of the original input is discarded as unsuitable.

At the neck of the funnel the deputy commissioner of education reviews acceptable proposals and consolidates them into a draft program. Substantive material is accompanied by legal opinions as well as notes for drafting the bills that would be necessary. Tentative priorities are assigned to each proposal and the program is sent to the commissioner of education and the board for final action.

The board's review is made with the advice of the commissioner and his deputy. Proposals that survive this final scrutiny emerge from the small end of the funnel as the regents' legislative program for transmission to the legislature, the governor, and the public.

From Program to Legislation

There are two major factors that make the regents and the State Education Department a force in the legislative process. First, the Board of Regents is constitutionally empowered to act in the field of education. Once the legislature has passed a statute the board draws up the policies and regulations for its administration. Politically the governor and the legislature are generally satisfied with this arrangement. If the board wants a piece of legislation it must be willing to stand the consequences of the expense of administering it and the public criticism it might produce. Thus, particularly when there is no funding attached or additional appropriation required by the department, the bill can easily clear the legislature. If there is some threat of major political repercussions that would affect the governor or the legislative leaders the proposal might be modified by the legislature before it is passed.

The second major factor is the vast amount of data and information that the department has available to put behind the regents' requests. The governor and the legislature recognize the high qualifications of the department in this regard. There is no other source for much of the information about the public schools, their programs, and costs. Neither the legislature nor the office of the governor can duplicate the technical services required to gather such data. The research offices of such organizations as the New York State Teachers Association have the capacity to supply only a fraction of the information. The governor's staff relies on the state education department data in developing the governor's program. Legislative committees and individual legislators also turn to the department for information. If the committees or individual legislators plan to make proposals, they do so essentially from the same basic data on which the regents and the governor are operating.

The liaison between the department and both the office of the governor and the legislature in bringing the regents' program to fruition has been very carefully assigned to particular people within the department hierarchy. The deputy commissioner is in over-all charge of legislative program strategy. The commissioner usually meets with the governor on request or when the commissioner feels it might be necessary. These meetings usually revolve around larger policy questions, especially finances. The department's law division, particularly the counsel, takes responsibility for conducting the relationships with the governor's counsels, particularly in legal matters and policy implications. The department counsel is also available for conversations with legislative committee counsels and committee chairmen.

The law division drafts most of the bills that make up the department program. It also reviews proposed legislation filed by legislators on their own initiative or at the request of groups outside of government. The law division can thus give technical assistance to legislators while it reviews proposed legislation for its effects on regents' policies or programs.

The executive assistant to the commissioner of education has the task of working with individual legislators. He not only undertakes to explain the regents proposals to legislators but also meets with legislators to explain why certain bills pertaining to education are undesirable in the view of the department. When other opinions are needed, in special areas such as vocational education, for example, it rests with the deputy commissioner to designate the department official who will conduct discussions with interested legislators or legislative committees. Relationships with the leadership in the legislature, including committee chairmen, rest largely with the deputy commissioner. He handles most routine matters, but makes judgments as to when he should suggest the commissioner's personal touch.

The Governor. If there is one central thrust to the role of the regents in educational policy-making in New York State, it is to have its proposals accepted by the governor as part and parcel of his program. Where he does follow the advice of the educational government he can count on the department to carry this message to the legislature and back it with appropriate, necessary, and factual data. Where the governor does not incorporate regents' proposals fully into his program he can expect to find opposition in the legislature insofar as the department can build support for the regents' program among legislative leaders and individual legislators. The regents realize that in a showdown over policy change the governor stands a better chance of winning in the legislature if he brings his political forces to bear. Thus, only when the gravest differences appear betweeen the regents' proposals and the governor's program is an open battle likely to take place.

The regents view Governor Rockefeller as a friend of education. His support of the state university system and increases in aid to the public schools from less than $500 to $860 per pupil during his four terms in office are cited as evidence of this support. The governor also has supported the regents' efforts to give special aid to the cities. The board is aware, however, that because he didn't press hard for the regents' original request for $100 million in 1968, the legislature appropriated only $26 million. Again, in 1969 when the governor proposed a 5 percent cut in school aid and downward revision of the aid formulas, the board was left in an embarrassing political position, having already endorsed a tax increase. Its relationship with the governor, however, has continued on the whole to be friendly and cooperative.

The Legislature. The Board of Regents is viewed with some apprehension by the legislature. The term "fourth branch of

77

government" has a negative connotation among legislators, according to a senate staff member. Legislators complain that the board proposes changes that cost money but escapes the onus of having to raise the revenues. While they have appreciated recent regents' endorsements of tax increases, legislators do not perceive these endorsements as taking political risks because members of the board do not have to gain approval by the voters. More recently regents' pronouncements on issues such as racial balance in the schools have, in the eyes of legislators, made it more difficult for them to support board proposals and still maintain voter support at home.

Even more disconcerting to legislators are the actions of the commissioner of education both in his role as advisor to the regents and his role as executor of regents' policies. The commissioner's regulations and decisions in public school matters were often attacked on the floor of the legislature as "highhanded" actions of a "virtual czar of education." Many legislators felt that the late James E. Allen, Jr., commissioner from 1955-69 and his educational bureaucracy captured the board and made it a virtual rubber stamp for his proposals. Criticism of Allen in this regard was prevalent as he approved mental health curriculums, ordered boards of education to integrate their schools, and moved to extend students' rights and privileges.

Curiously, however, the legislature has never moved directly to curtail Allen's power or that of any commissioner since the office was created in 1904. The reason for this is quite simple. In spite of what legislators might say, it is convenient to have a powerful commissioner to move schools in directions of which legislators approve but would dare not legislate. Thorny political items can be put in the hands of the regents or the commissioner as administrative items under the authority of the regents. Plans for redistricting the schools of the state, for example, affect every legislator. While the legislature has the authority to redistrict, it has consistently turned the task over to the regents and the commissioner for implementation. This occurred in 1948, 1957, and 1964 as legislative committees recommended and extended a state master plan for school district consolidation.[9] The only redistricting that has been fought out in the legislature was the decentralization of the New York City school system in 1968, 1969, and 1970. This came about as the constituents and interest groups in the City made it clear that their legislators would have to stand up and be counted on the question (See Chapter 7).

Educational Interest Groups

The relationship between the regents and educational interest groups has been a long one and for the most part cordial. The board's steadfastness in seeking increased state support giving more local tax relief is one basis for this good feeling. Its striving to preserve local control of schools and, at the same time, to provide insulation from partisan political wrangling at the state level is another. These postures have fostered a high degree of cooperation between the educational government and organizations such as the New York State School Boards Association, the New York State Teachers Association, and the Educational Conference Board.10

As Conant pointed out, the regents have not captured the interest groups nor have the interest groups captured the board.11 They have, instead, developed joint consultation and cooperation. The Educational Conference Board (ECB) is an excellent sounding board for department proposals in school finance. Representatives of the education department meet with representatives of the Educational Conference Board to inform them of the effects of the governor's program and the regents' proposals and to compare them with ECB proposals. In addition, the professional organizations are consulted regarding their views on changes in teacher certification and, at times, on matters of curriculum. The New York State School Boards Association and the New York State Council of School District Administrators are often consulted about impending changes in regulations or legislative proposals. Indeed, the school superintendents have continuing contact with education department officials through the commissioner's advisory council and legislation is always the topic of their January meeting. For their part, the interest groups have generally kept the department informed of their proposals for legislation on education. The basic approach of the schoolmen has been to avoid surprises and the triggering of almost reflexive negative bureaucratic reactions. Information gathered by the groups is shared with the department, at least to the extent that it supports the groups' points of view. When the groups and the educational government agree on proposed changes in state policy they act in concert to convince the governor and the legislature to make the changes.12

It is difficult to predict the next phase of the relationship between the interest groups and the regents. For reasons that will be presented in the next chapter, there is an air of impending change surrounding educational interest groups. Their interorganizational ties might soon snap or dissolve, fragmenting the coalition. For the regents this would be an unhappy but not disastrous turn of events. The new political style of the board will permit it to continue developing political strategy independent of education lobby groups.

* * *

The emerging role of the Board of Regents in the educational policy process is a more active political one. The board has sharpened the activities by which policy changes are developed and proposed. The State Education Department hierarchy is organized for active participation in the policy process with the legislature and with the governor's staff. While these changes have not greatly modified the governor's strategy for education nor the legislature's perception of the board, it has increased the potential for greater change in the future.

6

EDUCATIONAL
INTEREST GROUPS

Policy-making is not limited to actors who play formal roles in state government. Others, outside of the formal structure of government, play critical roles in this process. The goal of these actors, the interest group leaders,* is to move policy-makers toward decisions that favor the preferences and needs of their constituents. They play a legitimate and central role in the policy-making process, assuring that proposals that are the result of the idea formulation and debate stages of the Present-Preferred Cycle (described in Chapter 1) find their way into the course of deliberation and decision by actors holding formal positions in government. Their roles are vital in a democratic society. As Charles E. Lindbom observes, they "will be listened to with respect not because they wield power but because they are perceived to be representative of interests entitled . . . to be heard and to be accorded consideration. . . ."[1]

This chapter will focus on the roles of interest group leaders and, in particular, on the roles of educational interest group leaders at the state level. A framework for viewing interest groups will be developed and the bases of their influence will be explored. Next, the most influential educational interest groups in New York State will be identified and strategies that leaders of these groups employ to influence policy-makers will be described. Finally, responses

---

*Interest group leaders are often referred to as lobbyists and pressure group leaders. For practical purposes "interest groups generally undertake in some degree the activities originally covered by the noun 'lobby' . . . and by 'pressure groups.' " Graham Wootton, Interest-Groups (Englewood Cliffs, New Jersey: Prentice-Hall, 1970), p. 19.

of legislators concerning the effectiveness of these influencing techniques will be cited and contrasted to the views expressed by the
educational interest group leaders.

A FRAMEWORK FOR VIEWING INTEREST GROUPS

The interest groups analyzed in this study are those that have
persisted over time and have an intensive and limited focus on
educational policy concerns that results in persistent interaction
with state officials as they formulate educational legislation.

Persistence over Time

Interest groups vary not only in specific objectives but also in
their permanency and organizational forms. Interest groups vary
from anomic, spontaneous groups such as neighborhoods or university
students that organize around such short-range and immediate
phenomena as a riot or demonstration; to nonassociational groups
such as ethnic, regional, status, class, or kinship groups that lack
continuity or internal structure; to institutional groups such as
religious orders, skilled working groups, and official cliques; and,
finally, to associational groups such as trade unions and industrial
and civic groups, which have explicit representation, professional
full-time staffs, and orderly procedures.[2]
Educational interest groups can be found at all points of the
anomic-associational continuum. On the anomic end of the continuum
is the spontaneous movement of blacks in New York City who rose
up as a group to demand that the public school system be decentralized,
but disbanded as their demand was at least partially met. At the
other end of the continuum is the New York State Educational Conference Board, organized in 1934, which is an ongoing coalition of the
major educational interest groups in the state.
The educational interest groups that were initially selected for
analysis were those that, at the time of the study, could be characterized as associational. This narrowed the number of interest
groups to be explored, but still left more than a dozen possible groups,
including those representing teachers, administrators, board members, Parent-Teachers Associations, and several citizens' organizations. At this point the second criterion, scope and depth of
interest, was applied to these groups.

Intensive and Limited Focus

Wallace S. Sayre and Herbert Kaufman have devised a useful typology that classifies interest groups according to the scope and intensity of their participation in government affairs.[3] The typology classifies interest groups in four quadrants.

Quadrant I—high political intervention and broad political interest—includes relatively few nongovernmental actors. It is limited to a few civic groups and to the mass media that monitor the activities of government officials. Quadrant II—high political intervention and narrow political interest—includes those groups that display "high persistence in relatively narrow segments of the whole spectrum of political action."[4] These actors focus on such specific substantive areas of governmental activity as commerce, highways, welfare, or education and interact frequently with government officials. Quadrant III—low political intervention and narrow political activity—includes actors whose participation is sporadic and whose membership is constantly changing. Quadrant IV—low political intervention and broad political interest—is basically unpopulated unless one were to consider for inclusion such groups as the debating club at the corner bar.

We are particularly concerned with those interest group actors who fall within Quadrant II. These actors might "play a role in fewer decisions than any group in the first quadrant," but they "may well have greater influence on a particular decision within their special area of competence than any group in any quadrant."[5] These actor groups, for purposes of the present study, include those that are well-defined, those that have persisted over time, and those whose activities are both intense and highly focused on educational policy-making.

EDUCATIONAL INTEREST GROUPS

The criteria of persistence over time and intensity and focus of interest led to the selection of the groups depicted below as those interest groups most critical to the educational policy-making process at the state level in New York. Preliminary identification was made after reviewing past studies of educational interest groups in New York (especially Bailey and Usdan[6]). This was followed by discussions with legislative leaders and officials in the executive branch of the state government concerning the most important educational interest groups. There was general agreement that the following six educational interest groups are the relevant "others" who associate with state officials in the policy-making process.

FIGURE 2

Classification of Nongovernmental Groups by Scope of
Political Interest and Frequency of Political Intervention
in Governmental Decision-Making

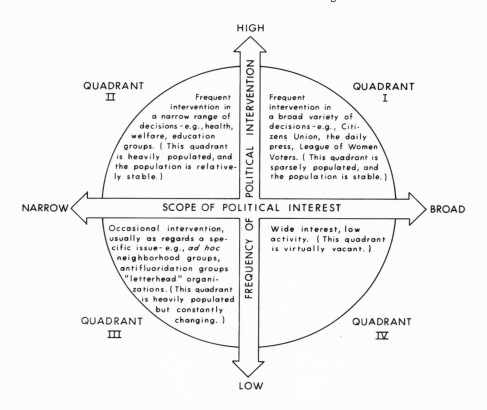

Source: From Chart 7, in Governing New York City by Wallace
S. Sayre and Herbert Kaufman, (C) 1965 by Russell Sage Foundation,
New York. By permission, W. W. Norton.

The Conference of Large-City Boards of Education
(Big Five)*

The so-called large city school districts in New York (classified
as such under the education law as cities over 125,000 population),

---

*This organization was formerly known as the Big Six. Results
of the 1970 census showed one of the member cities, Albany, falling
below the 125,000 population floor that is required if a city is to be

consist of New York City, Buffalo, Rochester, Syracuse, and Yonkers—
the "Big Five". These cities have two things in common that draw
them together as natural allies at the state level. First, by state
law they are fiscally dependent school districts. That is, the school
government in each of these cities must submit a budget to the mayor
and compete with other agencies for city revenues. Second, most
of the state's educationally and economically deprived young people
live in these cities. The magnitude of their educational needs and
the requirements for special programs that can meet these needs
often lead the big cities to seek special financial aid and unique
programs from the state legislature. Recognizing their common
needs, the large cities began in 1958 to meet at least annually and
in 1967 established a formal office in Albany to represent their
interests before the legislature and governor. By the latter date it
had become clear that other educational interest groups were not
going to direct many of their efforts toward pressing the legislature
to help large cities overcome their unique problems. As an interest
group the Big Five speaks for member school boards and administrators, but not for teachers or municipal governments.

New York Council
of School District Administrators (NYCSDA)

The NYCSDA, a relatively new organization, was organized in
1964. Its predecessor, the Council of City and Village Superintendents,
founded in 1883, did not include district superintendents and supervising principals.* As a result of the 1964 reorganization these
administrators have been brought into the new group and the chief
school officers of the state feel that they are in a better position to
play a persuasive role in the state's educational policy-making
process.

---

considered large under New York State law. Thus Albany was dropped
from the organization's membership.

*Also left out were elementary and secondary principals groups,
each of which has long had its own organizational framework. Although
not members in the NYCSDA, their voices have been joined with those
of the chief school officers in a new administrator's umbrella organization, the Congress of New York State School District Administrators,
founded in 1970.

New York State
School Boards Association (NYSSBA)

Since the NYSSBA's foundation in 1919 its major effort in legislative activity has been to reduce the incidence of taxation in local school districts and shift the burden of financing education to the state. At the same time it has been concerned with obtaining the greatest possible autonomy for local school boards in their operation of school districts. In this manner NYSSBA feels that it enhances the possibility that educational programs can be locally developed and operated.

New York State
Teachers Association (NYSTA)

The NYSTA, founded in 1845, is the oldest continuing state organization of teachers in the United States. The thrust of its legislative activity has been to improve the working conditions and welfare of teachers at the local district level. One means of accomplishing these ends has been to seek state policy change by legislation. As a result one of the major efforts of NYSTA takes place during the legislative session and is concentrated at the state capital. NYSTA, which can be characterized as upstate in membership and orientation, is the largest of the educational interest groups. Dues from its membership enables the organization to maintain a large and well-staffed office at the state capital. Much of the research and information disseminated by the educational interest groups is collected and developed by NYSTA staff members. The effects of the 1972 merger with United Teachers of New York (UTNY) on long established NYSTA activities remains to be seen.

New York State Educational Conference Board
(Educational Conference Board)

Three of the groups noted above, NYCSDA, NYSSBA, and NYSTA, are members of a coalition founded in 1934 called the Educational Conference Board (ECB). Other organizations that belong to the ECB include the New York State Congress of Parents and Teachers, the Public Education Association of New York City, the New York State Association for Secondary School Principals, the New York State Association for Elementary School Principals, and the New York State Association of School Business Officials. However, NYCSDA, which represents chief school officers, NYSSBA, which represents school boards, and NYSTA, which represents teachers are the most important and active members of this coalition organization. The Big Five, a recently developed organization, has a working relationship with the ECB but prefers to abstain from full membership because of the cities' unique needs. UTNY, geographically limited in its membership to urban areas and in particular to New York City, is a challenge to NYSTA as the voice of teachers and thus has not been welcomed as a member of the ECB. Whether this policy will change with the recent teachers' organizations merger is yet to be seen.

The major function of the ECB is to provide a place in which its several member organizations can put aside their differences and join together in common cause to seek improvements in the state's financing of education. Where agreements can be reached it is possible for member groups to speak with one voice when petitioning the state legislature and the governor's office in the cause of financing public education. In the past the ECB has been a very effective coalition, identifying and documenting education's financial needs for the governor, the legislature, and its own member organizations. Its proposals have been generally well-grounded in studies of the financial conditions of school districts and the costs of education.* There is reason to believe, however, that the effectiveness of the ECB is diminishing because of its refusal to deal with the critical needs of education in urban areas and because of the growing chasm between teachers and the other ECB constituent groups. These factors threaten to impair the ability of educational interest groups to cooperate in their dealings with state officials.

United Teachers of New York (UTNY)

UTNY is the state-level AFL-CIO teachers' umbrella organization. It is dominated by the United Federation of Teachers (UFT), the New York City teachers AFL-CIO affiliate, which provides the majority of UTNY membership as well as the leaders for the state-level organization. The teacher union movement is relatively new to the interest group scene in education. The UFT was founded in

---

*The ECB employed the research and leadership abilities of Paul Mort, a Columbia University Teachers College professor until his death in 1962. Other talented researchers have followed since this time, especially Lorne H. Woollatt of the State Education Department and Arvid J. Burke of NYSTA and the State University of New York at Albany.

1960.* Before its foundation positions taken before the legislature and with the ECB on behalf of New York City were carried by a progressive reform group, the Public Education Association of New York City (PES). With the decline of PES and the rise in militancy and membership of the UFT, this situation has changed. Since about 1963 it must be said that the UFT represents New York City teachers in state education policy matters and has become the leading voice among all New York City groups that monitor state activities. The UFT's rapid rise to a position of influence and the establishment of UTNY has challenged the UFT's much larger rival teachers organization, NYSTA for leadership in the teachers' drive to improve their economic and professional positions in school districts. (UTNY and NYSTA actually merged in 1972.) As a result of this challenge, relationships between the educational interest groups remain under severe stress.

STRESS ON THE INTEREST GROUP COALITION

A coalition base like the one ECB provides for educational interest groups is but one of several possible structural formats. Iannaccone visualizes four distinct educational interest group structural formats.**
1. Disparate (locally-based). Loyalties are school district-based and most interactions among schoolmen and legislators take place around these geographical lines. When educators do come together to fight for common programs, it is only with extreme difficulty. Vermont and New Hampshire are representative of this structural format.
2. Monolithic (state-wide). Interest groups representing the major constituencies exist at the state level and often work in unison to accomplish mutually agreed upon objectives. This format usually includes an "apex" linking organization that provides for communication and shared decision-making among the groups. New York and New Jersey are representative of this structural format.
3. Fragmented (state-wide). As in the Monolithic format there are interest groups at the state level. Under this format, however, they rarely speak with a unified voice. More often they are in

---

*The New York City Teachers Guild (AFT) and the High School Teachers Association merged into the UFT.
**From the book Politics in Education by Laurence Iannaccone, C 1967 by the Center for Applied Research in Education and used with their permission. (See especially pp. 38-82.)

conflict with each other as they jockey for a favored position among legislators. Michigan is representative of this structural format.

4. Syndical (state-wide). In this instance interest groups are linked directly to the legislature through a formal governmental unit. This type of structure includes legislators, governor's appointees, and ex officio members. The only example of this structural format is Illinois, where there are 10 legislators, five qubernatorial appointees (usually key educational interest group leaders), and, as an ex officio member, the superintendent of public instruction.

New York is an example of a Monolithic interest group structural format. Severe stress has been put upon this Monolithic structure, however, since Iannaccone wrote in 1967. In fact, it is very possible that New York's educational interest group structural format might soon approximate a Fragmented format more closely than a Monolithic format. The underlying reasons for this possible major change in format would be the Educational Conference Board's reluctance to deal with emerging educational needs and increasing teacher militancy, which is driving a wedge between teachers and other educational interest groups.

The Conference Board and Emerging Educational Needs

Usdan has noted that "there is still a great deal of respect for the Conference Board and its constituent organizations, however, there is a widespread feeling that these upstate Albany based organizations lack a 'sense of urgency' in articulating school issues."7 If anything, this feeling has grown stronger in the years since Usdan made this comment.

In particular, criticism has been leveled against the Educational Conference Board (ECB) for not exercising vigorous leadership in bringing the plight of the cities to the state's attention. As city schools have deteriorated, both physically and in their ability to meet the educational needs of an increasingly lower socioeconomic clientele, demands have increased on the ECB to lead efforts to seek relief for city school systems through state action. The ECB, a basically upstate body, has not responded to these demands in any significant way, mainly because it has achieved success in the past by supporting state financial programs that are to the benefit of all its member organizations. This time-tested formula has worked in the past but might not be adequate in coming years. (When questioned on this strategy at a 1969 ECB meeting, one of the directors of the coalition commented that "there is no reason to change. . . . W[e] will continue as we have in the past.") As members of the ECB come to view that umbrella organization as unable or unwilling to aid in their campaign for relief by the state, they might well splinter off and carry on many of their interest group activities independently.*

There are indications that this might already be happening. The Big Five, representing the school boards and administrators of the state's largest cities, has abstained from joining the ECB so as to keep urban-oriented needs clearly identifiable. It has established its own Albany office to monitor and influence activity of the state legislature and the governor, cooperating with the ECB when it is to its advantage to do so, but striking out independently when urban needs are being debated in the legislature or being considered by the governor.

Increasing Teacher Militancy

Militancy, a strident aggressiveness in seeking improved job conditions, has spread through the ranks of teachers in the United States in little more than a decade. In the wake of this movement cooperative relationships among teachers, administrators, and school boards have been severely strained. This movement has particularly affected such relationships in New York State. As Usdan observes:

> The United Federation of Teachers . . . in New York City is undeniably, the 'Big Bertha' of organized labor's efforts to unionize American teachers. As the largest and most influential local of the American Federation of Teachers (AFT), its dramatic contract victories in recent years have attracted national attention. Whether one agrees or disagrees with the pressure tactics employed, there is little doubt about the attractiveness to many teachers of the increases in salary and fringe benefits and the improvement in working conditions achieved by the union in New York City. Like its national counterpart, the N.E.A., the New York State Teachers Association (NYSTA) has reacted to the challenge of the union by becoming more militant itself. Threatened by the teachers union's recent gains, NYSTA . . . has exercised more muscle and its affiliates have become more aggressive in articulating the interests of teachers to school boards

---

*One constituent interest group leader bluntly told the authors that "the Educational Conference Board is burning out. . . . It has been coasting since 1962. . . . it has not kept up with the members' interests."

and administrators throughout the state. This teacher militancy in an increasing number of communities and on the state level as well is driving wedges between the teachers and their school boards and administrators.8

After a long period of resistance to the tactics employed by the UFT, the NYSTA has found that it must become more militant in its relations with school boards and administrators or risk a depletion of its membership, which is highly impressed by the gains won by the UFT for its teachers. The aggressiveness that NYSTA local affiliates have demonstrated in recent years, especially during contract talks, indicate that this organization has chosen to change its image to one that more closely approximates that of the UFT.

As a result of the changes in tactics employed by the NYSTA, the differences between it and the UTNY have become less apparent. In fact, by 1972 these two teachers organizations were able to agree to a merger. The new organization, the New York Congress of Teachers, is the result of extensive negotiations between the leaders of the two groups, Albert Shanker of the UTNY and Thomas Hobart of the NYSTA. The result of these negotiations has been the first unified union and professional teachers' organization in the nation.

It is possible that this merger will bring all teachers under the ECB umbrella. It is more likely, however, that it will be all the more difficult for teachers to agree with school boards and administrators on state educational policy-making objectives. Teachers might tend to focus more upon job conditions, while boards and administrators are left with the task of constraining these teacher efforts to minimize the impact on already strained local fiscal bases.

If such a wedge is irrevocably driven between teachers, administrators, and boards, the coalition in New York State will lose much of its influence. This is especially true because the ECB depends on the NYSTA, the largest and most wealthy of the member organizations, for much of its research, as well as information collection and dissemination activities.

Such stresses as those noted above will make it more difficult for educational interest groups to come to strategy and goal agreements before interacting with the legislature and the governor. Instead, there will probably be an increasing incidence of conflicting demands coming from the educational interest groups that will have to be resolved within the legislature or in the governor's office.

In short, it appears that educational interest groups in New York are undergoing a major structural modification, moving from the Monolithic format to the Fragmented format depicted by Iannaccone. If the ECB is not able to seize the initiative by taking positions on the emerging educational needs of the cities and by finding a way to overcome the gap between teachers, administrators, and boards, this will indeed be the case. One can expect that the future of New York State educational interest group activities will be depicted by more open politics, with groups taking their cases directly to formal government policy-makers for resolution rather than first trying to come to intergroup agreements. Such open politics will be marked by competition more than the present cooperation.

INFLUENCING MECHANISMS THAT CAN BE USED BY EDUCATIONAL INTEREST GROUPS

Whether Monolithic or Fragmented in structural format educational interest groups must have access to influence mechanisms of influence leverage on government officials to gain favored treatment for their constituents. That is, their potency in the policy-making process is highly dependent on their ability to employ influencing mechanisms that are recognized by governmental officials as legitimate and relevant inputs in their deliberations. These mechanisms include the control of information, the expert status ascribed to educators, the importance of children, and the power of the vote.

Control of Information

Until very recently educational interest groups held a virtual monopoly on information needed by legislators to make policy decisions. There were two reasons for this. First, educators are looked upon as having special expertise that makes them uniquely qualified to gather and analyze such information. Second, state governments, and especially state legislators, have been operating with minimum support staff, reducing the possibility of meaningful audits of this information.*

Because its availability is limited information is a valued resource. Those who possess information are in an excellent position to influence policy-makers. As one state legislator noted in an earlier survey, interest groups "can study and present the issues concisely—the average legislator has no time or inclination to do this and wouldn't understand bills or issues without them. A

---

*State governments are beginning to be more fully staffed. As this proceeds the dominant position of the interest groups as controllers of information will probably be significantly challenged by executive agencies and legislative committees.

professional lobbyist in ten minutes can explain what it would take
a member two hours to wade through just reading bills."9 Interest
groups, of course, must provide accurate and complete information
if they are to expect government officials to trust their inputs.

Expert Status Ascribed to Educators

Educators have persuasively argued that their long years of
professional training and experience in educating children puts them
in the best position to make decisions in matters related to educational
policy-making. For the most part lay citizens and government
officials alike have accepted this argument. Educational interest
groups have used this special status to advance their proposals.
There probably will be less willingness on the part of government officials to acquiesce in the views of educators than in the past.
This is due in part to the fact that state governments are being up-
graded. More qualified people are being attracted to state service
as a result of improved salary structures and the growing role of
state government. As a result, educators are often confronted by
government officials who are more knowledgeable about educational
issues than they are. It is also due however, to the shaken belief
that educators can adequately handle educational problems. The
failure of educators to meet the challenge posed by lower socio-
economic groups in the inner core of our cities has enhanced this
skepticism.

The Importance of Children

Children might be the most valuable influencing "mechanism"
available to educational interest groups. In a nation as child-oriented
as the United States it is difficult to conceive of organized groups
working against supporting the education of children. Those few
groups that do come out against extending state aid to education are
very careful to use such terms as "frugality," "efficiency," and
"taxpayer limitations." Educational interest groups in New York have
used children as an influencing mechanism on policy-makers very
successfully. Educators, who freely admit to the use of this technique,
feel that it puts them in a distinctly advantageous position over
interest groups lobbying for such areas as welfare and old age
assistance. Partially as a result of the use of this influence mechanism
the level of support for education by the state has been consistently
high, despite a relatively large parochial school population (15.4
percent of all school-age youth).

Finally, the power of the vote can be a highly potent influencing mechanism for educational interest groups. Labor, as an interest group, is most able to use this mechanism because its membership is quite broad and its affiliated groups e.g., members' families and their friends) are large in number. Educational interest groups can also be important vote getters, however, and legislators seem to be increasingly aware of this in New York State. Group membership is quite extensive. By the 1970-71 school year there were 213,492 professional staff members in the state's public schools. Teachers alone accounted for 185,223 of these positions.[10] Even more important, however, is the possibility that local citizens can be influenced by school boards, administrators, and teachers to vote for or against their local legislator depending upon his position on educational issues. This has not been extensively tested, but might well be a device more often used by education interest groups as states continue to increase their support of public education.

Educational interest groups employ the above four mechanisms to influence public officials directly and indirectly as they deliberate educational policy matters. Direct influence includes testifying before committee hearings, sending information brochures to the legislative chambers, calling on legislators, visiting the governor and his key lieutenants, and responding to inquiries made by government officials. Indirect influence includes instigating letter-writing campaigns to legislators by educators and other citizens, taking out advertising space in newspapers, using radio and television time, and organizing protest marches on the state capital. There is a variety of ways in which these influencing mechanisms can be applied. In the final analysis, however, it is the task of the leaders of educational interest groups to decide when and how to influence government officials. The extent to which interest groups succeed in obtaining "friendly" legislation is directly related to the ability of their leaders to influence the policy-making process.

It is important to describe how influence is actually applied if we are to know whether educational interest groups are effective lobbyists. We will now explore, therefore, first the self-reported influencing strategies of educational interest groups and second, the perceptions of legislators concerning the effectiveness of these strategies.

STRATEGIES FOR INFLUENCING EDUCATIONAL LEGISLATION

Table 6.1 presents, in capsule form, the results of interviews with educational interest group leaders concerning the educational policy-making process at the state level and the ways in which they operate to influence that process. Although the interest groups vary in purpose, they share several characteristics that can be explored. That is, there appear to be patterns of lobbying that hold constant across these groups, activities that, on the basis of experience, they feel will maximize their influence in the policy-making process.

Educational interest group leaders without exception saw the governor's office as the critical access point in the policy-making process. Several reasons were given by respondents for this conclusion. First, the governor, as a state-wide elected official, is in a position to bring state-wide considerations to bear on educational issues. Second, the governor is responsible for developing an executive budget that forecasts the state's fiscal needs and is the expression of his program for state growth and development. The budget becomes a major focus of legislative activity. Third, as the recognized leader of his party the governor can bring great influence to bear on his party's legislators.

Within the legislature itself educational interest group leaders focus their activities on the leadership. "Legislative leadership" is defined by interest group leaders as the speaker, the chairman of the Ways and Means Committee and the chairman of the Education Committee in the assembly and the majority leader, the chairman of the Finance Committee and the chairman of the Education Committee in the senate, as well as the minority leaders in both chambers. A secondary tactic, less universal in application, is to contact individual legislators in their home districts. Local influence activities are carried on by the interest groups' local organizations.

Most educational interest group leaders think that their most important influencing mechanism is the information-gathering and dissemination potential of their organizations. This is particularly true of the NYSTA, the ECB, and the Big Five. The basic assumption of these organizations is that through their unique ability to gather data state-wide and provide factual information to the governor and legislature they can influence the shaping and processing of educational legislation. Other educational interest groups, such as the NYSSBA and the NYCSDA, often rely on the data-gathering capacities of the above organizations rather than perform these costly research activities independently.

Responsibility for carrying out interest group activities appears to lie at both the state and local level. Most organizations have offices in Albany in which one or more individuals carry on the day-to-day activities of the organization, including visits with the governor's aides and the legislative leadership. At the same time it is expected that as organizational objectives concerning legislation develop the membership will apply pressure on their legislators at the grass-roots

95

TABLE 6.1

Selected Educational Interest Groups: Perceptions of the
Policy-Making Process

Educational Interest Groups	Objective	View of the Control Point in the Policy Process	Tactics Employed in Influencing the Legislative Process	Persons Responsible for Influencing Policy-Making
Conference of Large-City School Districts	Unique fiscal and programming needs of the large cities	Governor, mayors, and other city officials	1. Influence mayors and city officials to contact the governor. 2. Influence commissioner of education to contact governor. 3. Data-gathering for legislative leadership and key committees. 4. Data gathering for local boards and administrators to influence legislators.	Executive secretary
Council of School District Administrators	Similar to NYSBA with added special concerns for maintenance of their positions within the educational hierarchy	Governor: budget and program	1. CSDA convention to set legislative plans. 2. Reach legislative leadership and chairmen of key committees. 3. CSDA Advisory Board to influence commissioner of education. 4. Administrators talk with legislators in the districts.	1. President of the council. 2. Committee on Legislation. 3. Local administrators talk with their legislators.
New York State Educational Conference Board	Increased state support for education: encompasses needs that cross over those of individual member organizations	Governor: control of the Legislature	1. Studies of costs of education and the fiscal condition of school districts. 2. Development of programs for legislation. 3. Get program adapted by governor.	Constituent groups

Organization	Goal	Governmental target	Tactics	Access/Contacts
New York State School Boards Association	Relief of local school districts from burden of excessive financial support for education	Governor: executive budget, Division of Budget and Office of Local Government	1. Explain NYSBA program to governor and his counsels. 2. Reach legislative leadership and chairmen of key committees. 3. Talk with legislators in the districts. 4. Capture commissions set up by governor and legislature. 5. Various tactics developed due to diversity of membership.	1. Executive secretary and one or two key staff members. 2. Regionally and locally, school boards talk with legislators.
New York State Teachers Association	Improved working conditions and welfare of teachers	Governor: office and program	1. Reach legislative leadership and chairmen of key committees. 2. Supply information (extensive research capacity).	1. Executive secretary and one or two key staff members. 2. Letters from association members.
United Teachers of New York	Improving working conditions and welfare of teachers, especially in New York City	Governor, N.Y.C. mayor, and other city officials	1. Influence mayor and city government of New York City. 2. Influence N.Y.C. area legislators who then contact upstate legislature.	1. President of UFT. 2. Legislative representatives.

Source: Compiled by the authors.

level. In addition, urban-oriented educational interest groups attempt
to involve local government officials in pressing legislators and the
governor about the cities' educational needs.

Noted by omission is any extensive reference to the Board of
Regents as critical in the interest groups' influencing process. While
they view the board as a body that is able to move the legislature and
governor on desired educational policy, interest group leaders did
not indicate that they employ the regents in advancing their own causes.
They do meet with representatives of the regents to share information
at times ("joint consultation"), but this is as far as they cooperate.
Such responses would indicate that neither of these actor groups has
been able to capture the other and that each plays a relatively independent role in moving their respective legislative programs.[11]

In summary, the educational interest groups generally held these
perceptions: first, that the governor's office is the key access point
in the policy-making system; second, that the legislature is centrally
controlled by a few legislators who hold leadership positions within
it; third, that the educational interest groups' most potent weapon in
influencing the policy-making process is their ability to make
recommendations based upon data concerning educational policy; and
fourth, that interest group members maintain pressure on their
legislative representatives to achieve organizational objectives
concerning educational legislation, but major responsibility for
influencing the policy-making process is placed in the hands of one
or two interest group leaders who maintain contact with government
officials in Albany.

THE LEGISLATURE:
PERCEPTIONS OF THE POLICY-MAKING PROCESS
AND THE INFLUENCE OF INTEREST GROUPS

The ways in which the legislature goes about making policy
relate directly to behavioral norms that develop over time. Legislators operate within a set of real and imaginary constraints that
significantly affect how they view policy proposals and how they
interact with their fellow legislators and individuals outside the
legislative body. They are subject to much pressure from individuals
and groups both within and outside of the legislature. Within the
legislature they exchange information, ideas, and advice with their
colleagues, committee chairmen, and party leaders. They also
interact with executive agency personnel, interest group representatives, and various subgroups from their constituencies. All of these
groups and individuals bring influence to bear on legislators as they
debate and vote on educational issues. The question of import, then

is how close are the legislators' perceptions of the policy-making system to those of the educational interest groups? Further, how do legislators view the influencing strategies of educational interest groups? To test these questions it might be useful to organize perceptions of legislators around the four major conclusions about influencing strategies drawn from interviews with educational interest group leaders.

The Governor's Office as the Access Point in the Policy-Making Process

The educational interest group leaders felt that the most critical point of entry in the policy-making process is the governor's office. Legislators, on the other hand, felt that the governor's influence is not nearly so great. A substantial minority of legislators (41 percent) reported that they give the governor's position little or no attention when voting on bills. Forty-two percent felt that consideration of the governor's position depends on the specific policy issue in question.

When asked to rank the importance of specific groups on their views about educational laws legislators ranked the executive agencies eighth out of nine groups (see Table 6.2). Legislators ranked their own expert colleagues (i.e., legislators who specialize in educational finance and other educational areas) as the most important group influencing their views on educational legislation. It should be noted that several groups, including the interest groups, were ranked far ahead of the executive agencies. It might be argued that the governor and the executive agencies cannot be equated, but the influence the governor has over these agencies through his appointive powers and budgetary control makes for a strong and direct relationship between them. Many legislators noted that they consider these agencies to be extensions of the governor's office.

When the governor was perceived as influential, legislators believed this influence was based upon his veto power (44 percent); relationships with his party's leadership in the legislature (36 percent); and the patronage at his disposal (32 percent). Interestingly, whereas educational interest group leaders felt that one of the critical influence bases available to the governor is his close relationship with the legislative leadership, only 9 percent of legislators responding to the survey felt that legislative leaders play a significant role in overseeing the governor's program.

TABLE 6.2

Groups Influencing Legislators' Views on Educational
Legislation
(in percent)

Groups	Legislators Noting Group as "Very Important" Influencers[a]
Experts in the Legislature	55
People in the Districts	48
Education Committees	39
Educators Back Home	34
Educational Interest Groups	25
Legislative Staff Opinions	24
Committees other than Education	14
Executive Agencies	8
Party Leaders	6

[a]The number of respondents who ranked these influencers varied from 100 to 103 across the nine choices.

Source: Compiled by the authors.

The Legislature as a Highly Centralized
Policy-Making Body

Educational interest group leaders reported that they concentrate activities within the legislature on the recognized leadership in each chamber because they view the legislature as a highly centralized policy-making body. Again, there were wide differences in the way educational interest group leaders and legislators viewed the legislature's operations. While 38 percent of responding legislators indicated that the leadership controls party members and states the party position, very few legislators (9 percent) viewed the legislative leaders as overseers of the governor's program. Also, as noted in Table 6.2, only 6 percent of the responding legislators felt that the party leaders influence their decisions concerning pending legislation.

Additional data indicate a wide perceptual discrepancy between legislators and interest group leaders concerning the degree to which the legislature is a centralized decision-making body. A highly centralized legislative body requires that parties maintain tight discipline among their members. Only 38 percent of the responding legislators, however, agreed that there is tight party discipline.

Sixteen percent felt that whether party discipline is enforced depends upon the issue at hand, that is, whether there is a party position. Most legislators acknowledged that they consider the views of their party leaders before they vote on a bill, but 32 percent noted that the critical factor in considering the party leaders' position is whether the bill is a party measure. A majority of the respondents felt that there are times when a legislator should not vote with his party. In particular, most legislators believed, he should be free to vote the dictates of his conscience (55 percent) and give preference to his district's needs over those of his party when the two conflict (59 percent).

Few legislators (14 percent) felt that it is necessary to speak with the chamber's leadership to assure the successful passage of a bill. Legislators reported that they seek out the views on a bill of other legislators who have good judgment and general knowledge or seniority and expertise, whether they belong to the chamber's leadership or not. In reality the legislature's committee system tends to dilute the influence of the leadership. Legislators must bring proposed legislation for study, review, and approval to the appropriate committee before it may reach debate and voting on the chamber's floor. The committee chairman plays a crucial role in the committee structure. Legislators felt (40 percent) that he is able to foster or hinder the movement of a bill. In fact, 24 percent of the responding legislators referred to the chairman as having "life or death" power over the destiny of a bill. It should be noted, however, that a similar number (26 percent) felt that the leadership controls the committees because the majority leaders assign bills and appoints committee chairmen. Nevertheless, 63 percent of the respondents recognized the fact that legislation is most expeditiously moved when legislators contact the appropriate committee chairman and/or members of that committee.

Educational Interest Groups' Use
of Information to Influence Legislators

No legislator can be an expert in more than a few substantive areas. Consequently it becomes important that sufficient information be made available if legislators are to understand measures on which they must vote. Educational interest groups view their ability to present complete and accurate data for consideration by legislators as a most important influencing mechanism. There are many sources to which legislators can turn for information concerning proposed legislation, however, both within and outside of the legislature. In fact, one staff member on the assembly's Ways and Means Committee told the authors that he had more than adequate information sources without using educational interest group information. A counsel to the majority leader in the senate noted that "information, especially in the area of education, is available in prodigious quantities." These comments are in direct opposition to the perceptions of interest group leaders.

When asked what they considered the most important sources of information available to legislators in studying the facts about bills, responding legislators noted in-house sources most frequently (see Table 6.3). Information from interest groups ranked second, but far behind information support arms within the legislature itself and just ahead of several other information sources, including others within the legislature. In the past several years the legislature in New York has developed sophisticated information-gathering systems to free itself of dependency on executive agencies and interest groups. Probably as a result of this, when asked where they might turn when it appears that no information is readily available on a measure, only one legislator said that he checks with interest groups for data. Actually interest groups ranked last in a list of 12 possible sources of information when it appeared that such information was not immediately at hand.

Influencing the Policy-Making Process: Interest Group Leaders and their Membership

Leaders of interest groups attempt to influence legislators in directions that favor the objectives of their organizations. Legislators spend much time in direct conversation with these group officials and in reading their literature. Eventually they must decide whether to take interest group positions into consideration when voting on legislation. Educational interest groups in New York see the collection and dissemination of data and representation by their leaders in Albany as their most potent influencing weapons. These groups also attempt to rally their members to influence legislators at the local level. Legislators' responses to the survey, however, would leave the effectiveness of the overall educational interest groups' strategy in some doubt.

According to responding legislators the three most powerful interest groups in New York are labor (79 percent), education (54 percent) and banking, finance and insurance (32 percent). Sixty-two percent feel that the size, or voting strength of an interest group is its most important power base. Money (29 percent), effective propaganda (25 percent), and good organization (20 percent) trailed far behind the membership size criterion. Educational interest group

TABLE 6.3

Sources of Information for Studying
the Facts About Bills
(in percent)

Sources	Legislators Noting Source (N=113)
Centralized Legislative Research Agencies	74
Interest Groups	24
Sponsor and Bill Memorandum	20
Executive Agencies	16
Counsels, Legislative Staff, Committee Reports	13
The Leadership	5
Mass Media	4
Other Members	3

Source: Compiled by the authors.

representatives can use their large constituency size to good effect. This has not been tested extensively in New York, but legislators appear to be cognizant of the potential of such a voting bloc.

The most powerful interest groups in education, according to legislators are the UFT (54 percent), the NYSSBA (26 percent), and the NYSTA (23 percent). Underlying the power of these specific groups, according to the responding legislators, are their voting strength (58 percent) and their knowledge-expertise-status bases (45 percent). This educational interest group ranking is somewhat surprising, given the fact that the NYSTA maintains a complex operation in the state capital, while the UFT focuses its resources at the local level in New York City, and its state level organization, the UTNY, plays a minimal role in Albany. An unexpectedly low-visibility group is the ECB (5 percent).

Thus legislators did not feel that the Albany-based operations of the interest groups were the most relevant influence mechanisms available to these groups. On the contrary, legislators were more concerned about the interest groups' membership at the local level.[12] As noted in Table 6.2, educators back home rank above the formal interest groups as influencers (34 percent-25 percent). "Educators back home" are, in reality, the local arms of the educational interest groups.

In summary then, the results indicate that there are critical differences in perceptions between educational interest group leaders and legislators regarding the policy-making process:

1. The governor's office as the key to the policy-making process. Educational interest group leaders perceive the governor and his executive agencies as the primary entry point in the policy-making process, particularly because of his legislative initiative. Legislators do not feel that the governor plays such an important role in this process and that his most potent influence is the veto power.

2. The legislature as a highly centralized body. Educational interest group leaders perceive the legislature as highly controlled by a leadership group that carries the governor's program. Legislators feel that these leaders exert much less influence than supposed by outsiders and that the leaders do not necessarily oversee the governor's program in the legislature, except when there is a party position or the measure being considered is a party bill.

3. Information as a potent interest group resource. Educational interest group leaders feel that their most important influencing weapon is access to information that can be used by legislators in the decision-making process. Legislators feel that there are many sources of information at their disposal. Interest group information is but one of these sources and often not the most important.

4. Representation of interest group concerns. Educational interest groups concentrate their activities in the hands of a few officials at the state capital and ask their members to influence legislators from their home districts. Legislators feel that groups, educational and noneducational, in their districts are more important than the formal interest groups' representatives at the state capital in influencing their actions.

POSSIBLE REASONS FOR PERCEPTUAL VARIATIONS

Why did educational interest group leaders and state legislators view the policy-making process so differently? One possible explanation might be the positions of these two groups in what Heinz Eulau calls the "stratification of political relations."[13] Eulau notes that "individuals or groups in neighboring strata are more likely to come into contact with each other than individuals or groups in widely different strata." This is especially true in a highly formal and relatively closed political system such as the New York state legislature. Thus legislators in their first or second term of office, as were about one-third of those responding to the survey, probably do not associate on a continuing or close basis with the formal leadership of the legislature or representatives of the governor's office.

They probably associate instead with other relatively new legislators. Educational interest group leaders, most of whom have been at the state capital for a decade or more, have a close working relationship with the legislative leadership and the governor's office. This is true partly because they have had many opportunities over the years to establish close personal contacts and partly because of the nature of their jobs. Their role is to influence these state officers, whereas the newer legislators' roles in the legislature do not encourage frequent contact with the leadership. It is logical, therefore, that these legislators would have perceptions of the policy-making process that differ from the views of educational interest group leaders.

Another possible explanation for the perceptual variations is that the policy-making process, which has traditionally been highly centralized in New York, might have undergone modifications in the past several years. There is some evidence that this is actually the case. The speakership changed hands in 1969. The incumbent, Speaker Duryea is viewed as more willing to decentralize powers among the committees and individual legislators than was his predecessor, who was characterized as autocratic and running a tightly-structured assembly. A similar change took place earlier in the majority leader's office in the senate. Educational interest group leaders who have long associated with a highly centralized legislature might not have been able to make the necessary shifts in perception.

Whether either of these explanations of perceptual variations is correct is not nearly so important as the fact that educational interest group leaders and state legislators view the policy process and ways of influencing that process very differently. So long as legislators believe that the process operates in a way different from that in which interest group leaders see it interest group strategies will remain less than optimally effective.

**TWO CASES OF
EDUCATIONAL
POLICY-MAKING
IN THE 1969
LEGISLATIVE SESSION**

In this chapter the interplay of forces in the educational policy-making process will be illustrated in two cases. In both cases events, actors, and activities observed during the 1969 legislative session will be highlighted. Several themes presented in previous chapters will be explored: the ability of the governor to dominate the process and his strategies for handling regents' proposals, the role of legislative leaders in maintaining party discipline and finding compromises, the general reactions of legislators, and the activities of interest groups. Several uses of information will also be indicated. The first case focuses on the perennial concern for school finance and the governor's budget. The second case presents an emerging concern, the decentralization of city schools, and focuses on the situation in New York City.

SCHOOL AID AND BUDGET REDUCTION

State aid to public schools is a perennial concern of educators and politicians alike. Since the 1920s, when formulas for aid distribution were introduced in New York, there have been almost annual struggles between the two groups over increases in the appropriation and/or changes in the formulas of aid distribution. In almost every decade, state commissions or joint legislative committees have been appointed to review state educational finance policy and, at the same time, reduce or solve political difficulties of the governor and legislature. Educational interest groups have also conducted studies of school finance and utilized their findings to impress state officials with the needs of the schools. Ultimately, however, the final act is staged in the legislature during the annual battle of the budget.

Background to 1969

In 1962 a joint legislative committee, the Diefendorf Committee,* recommended a new basis for state aid distribution: the shared-cost concept whereby the state would pay a portion of every dollar expended by local districts in operating costs. The state portion, or aid ratio, would be based on a percentage of the difference between the district's taxable wealth per pupil and the average taxable wealth per pupil of all districts. The recommendation also included an immediate increase in the aid appropriation for the coming year.

This recommendation, based on expenditure decisions at the local school district level, appeared to legislators to be a raid in perpetuity on the state treasury. To prevent it the legislature put a ceiling of $500 on the per-pupil costs in which the state would share, making reconsideration of the ceiling necessary in succeeding legislative sessions. Governor Rockefeller, to salve the wounds of schoolmen, requested and got an aid appropriation for the coming year that was larger than the Diefendorf Committee recommended.[1]

By 1967 it was clear that state aid was not keeping pace with costs and, as a result, local tax burdens were increasing. In addition, school problems, especially in the cities, were becoming more acute and funds were needed to find solutions. The legislature turned to the Joint Legislative Committee to Revise and Simplify the Education Law (simplified to the acronym JLC) extending its authority to examine school aid policy. As the JLC was an unknown quantity in finance matters and seemed fully under the control of the leadership, the interest groups looked on this decision with trepidation. The recommendations of the JLC were for a $760 per-pupil aid ceiling, a reduction in transportation aid, and $100 million for a special urban aid program. The Educational Conference Board (ECB) opposed the reduction in transportation aid and called for a ceiling of $800. The regents also asked for the $800 ceiling and $112 million in urban aid. The governor's budget for 1968 proposed only $26 million for special aid to cities and a ceiling of $726. The ECB as well as the interest groups campaigned against these proposals. The governor compromised. He left it up to the legislature to choose so long as it did not raise taxes beyond increases he had proposed. The Republican majority was split, with upstate legislators seeking $700 and suburban and downstate delegations calling for the $800 figure. According to a former JLC staff member, the easiest way out was to accept the

---

*The Joint Legislative Committee on School Financing had both legislative and public members. One of the latter, Charles Diefendorf, a banker, was the chairman.

JLC recommendations, reduce other portions of the governor's program, particularly social welfare, and let the governor take the blame for the tax increases. This strategy was predicated on the fact that the legislature faced elections in November. Legislators wanted to go home having done well by education and keeping new taxation to a minimum by cutting welfare. The compromise outcome, however, also set the stage for a renewed aid struggle in 1969.

Scene-Setter

A deepening financial crisis in the state was outlined by Rockefeller at the opening of the 1969 legislature. Revenue was not keeping pace with program costs. His response to these problems was to impose a 5 percent cutback in all state spending. The cut was to be made across all programs without exception and coupled with an increase in the sales tax to produce the required balanced budget. For education there was an added blow in the form of proposed formula changes to reduce the state's share from 49 percent of each dollar expended to 46 percent. There were increases in the aid for districts with high tax rates, however, and urban aid was to continue at $52 million. In actual monies the governor was proposing to add $332 million for education over 1968, largely in special aids and high tax aid affecting some districts, while cutting operating aid, which affected all districts.[2]

The regents were already on record in favor of a $900 ceiling and a state share increase to 54 percent as well as a tax increase to pay for the added funding.[3] With the election of the legislature over and the gubernatorial election still nearly two years away it seemed to be a reasonable approach. In actuality, however, the Board of Regents was out on a political limb.

The ECB also sought a $900 ceiling and a state share of 54 percent. It seemed to the board to be fiscal chicanery on the part of the governor to cut basic operating aid and then give a 16 percent increase. While many schools would get less aid the governor could claim credit as having continued to help education in a year of austerity. But it was apparent that a campaign to attain $900 would be futile.

In the legislature reaction to the education proposals was mixed. Senate Majority Leader Earl Brydges told an interviewer that the regents' and the ECB's proposals were "out of the question." The governor's plan for meeting the state's problems, Brydges said, was a necessity. Assembly Speaker Perry Duryea, with only a six-vote Republican margin, indicated that the line would be held. The speaker's statement reflected the fact that his majority included 11 Republicans who had been elected on the Conservative party line as opponents of taxing and spending. Assembly Minority Leader Stanley Steingut, while agreeing that there was a fiscal crisis, felt that cuts in school aid were "very dangerous" and doubted that "any Democrat would vote for them." Nor would Democrats, he said, vote for added taxes.[4]

Meanwhile Senator Clinton Dominick, chairman of the JLC, decided to expose the cuts and formula changes for their eventual effect: a 15 percent cut in all education aid by 1970 and beyond. His exposure was an internal one, according to a former JLC staff member, made before legislators and legislative leaders; it did not involve the State Education Department nor educational interest groups.

Thus the roles of the major actors were cast. The governor had proposed his finance policy of reductions to the legislature. The legislative leadership was prepared to see it through insofar as it could keep the majority party in line while opposition to portions of the program came from the minority party. The regents had stated their position on policy improvement but had effectively been cut off by the governor's decision to reduce state spending. The educational interest groups had been prepared to lobby for a change in finance policy, but the positions of the governor and the legislative leadership forced them to lobby in defense of the current policy. The governor's proposed budget thus became the focal point for the legislative struggle.

The 1969 Session

The budget was sent to the legislature in mid-January. It did not take long for the interest groups to begin planning their activities when they saw the full dimensions of the proposed cuts. Legislators, for their part, seemed to be waiting for the counterproposals that might come from the interest groups, their own constituents, and the regents.

Educational Interest Groups

Educational Conference Board. The ECB mobilized to save the existing ceiling of $760 and the 49 percent sharing level. Bills for the proposed $900 ceiling, already drafted, were laid aside. The study of education needs for the 1970s, begun in 1968, was scanned for data to present in making a stand.[5] A new strategy was devised for reaching the members of the constituent organizations.

In an early February 1969 meeting observed by one of the authors action was planned to counter Rockefeller's proposals. State Education Department officials were on hand to explain what the cuts would mean. They indicated that the department would not openly join the ECB in working for the retention of $760. "We can't fight the governor on this one," said one official. "The legislature made it $760 last year and the governor will throw the crisis back on them." It was almost an admission that the regents' recommendations had been ignored and that further internal lobbying with the governor was useless.

ECB strategy was to indicate that the state was not providing its fair share of support to education Joint committees of teachers, administrators, and school boards in each school district were to carry the message. Worksheets were designed to show, for each district, the comparative effects of the aid cut, present aid, and the ECB's proposed increase on the local tax rate. The worksheets could be filled out by the schoolmen and then shown to local legislators accompanied by the unmistakable message that their votes for aid cuts would be votes for higher local school taxes.

The ECB also went on record in favor of the proposed sales tax increase. There was some thought that this support might be made conditional either on retention of present aid or on passage of an increase. Nothing definite was decided, however, and the original statement stood.

Clearly the ECB was out to stir up the countryside and put individual legislators in a squeeze with their constituents if they voted for school aid cuts. If this strategy worked it would bring legislators to the leadership asking for better treatment of education. The leaders, in turn, would seek to modify the governor's proposals so that members could go home with an education support package that kept local tax increases at a minimum. As ECB Chairman Kenneth Buhrmaster said at the close of the February meeting, "We will use the press and the local organizations to get up the legislators. The message is that the state is not carrying its share."

ECB Member Groups. In addition to ECB activities, the State Teachers Association, the School Board Association, and the administrators' organizations conducted their own campaigns "to save $760." Generally they all followed the ECB strategy to educate their members and reach legislators. Their elected officers put out news releases, spoke to various groups, and appeared before a joint hearing of the senate Finance Committee and the assembly Ways and Means Committee in mid-February.[6]

The executive staff members carried out their usual tasks of supplying local organizations with information and visiting with the chairmen of education and finance committees. The legislative bulletins of the teachers association and school boards association, issued weekly, kept their members informed of the progress of legislation as well as the organizations' positions on each bill.

In addition, the executive secretary of NYSTA sent a letter to all
legislators pointing out how the governor's proposals would reduce
school aid while showing an overall increase for education, resulting
in public misunderstanding.

The Big Six Cities. The Conference of Large City Boards of Education
had a different kind of problem in the view of its executive secretary,
Dwight Beecher. While the Big Six were represented in the legislature by 127 assemblymen and senators, 94 of these were from New
York City. The mayor of New York City had requested a large increase
for general municipal aid and there was some fear that the governor
might hold these legislators in line by tacitly exchanging their votes
on cuts for a better aid package for the City.

But Beecher also saw the 5 percent cut announcement as a ploy
by the governor to get new taxes and leave the onus of the increase
on the legislature. He felt the governor was saying to the legislature:
"If you want a program funded at a higher level I'll go along when it
is clear that you have raised taxes to pay for it."

Thus there were two messages for Big Six legislators: Hold
the line on per-pupil aid and special aids important to cities and vote
for the sales tax. There was little hope that the 83 Democrats in the
cities' delegations would fall in line on the sales tax, but their support
of the present aid ceiling could serve to make a solid front with other
legislators from rural and suburban districts. About 40 were already
so disposed because their legislative districts included suburban
schools.

Meanwhile the Big Six mayors, their superintendents, and their
school board presidents made the annual pilgrimage to Albany to meet
with the governor. Although no one changed his position, this provided
a public display of the urban plight to which the governor at least had
to give recognition.

The Regents

The regents realized that their legislative program had no
chance of emerging intact. The board was somewhat out on a limb,
having endorsed a tax increase that the governor could use as partial
support for his tax proposal. The best that could be hoped for was
an accommodation whereby the urban aid program would be continued
at about the same level as in the previous year and the ceiling on per-
pupil aid would hold at its present level. The State Education Department moved to carry out this compromise. Allen Bradley, executive
assistant to the commissioner, made the contacts with legislators.
Characterized by some legislators as the "personable old shoe,"
Bradley had taken up the day-to-day contact work about three years

earlier. In the summers of 1967 and 1968 he had visited many legislators at home to discuss "matters of mutual concern" away from the press of legislative business. These conversations included presentation of the regents' broad goals for education in the coming years. Now Bradley moved to prevent the 1969 budget crisis from scuttling progress toward these goals.

At the same time the commissioner of education and his deputy undertook the defense of the regents' proposals as submitted. This was done through joint hearings held by the legislative financing committees as well as through response to questions from the legislative leaders. These tactics were not unusual, for the department has generally felt free to reiterate its original proposals to the legislature while most other departments shift to endorsing the governor's budget as it pertains to their agency. The tactics for education were based on the relative independence of the regents from gubernatorial control as well as the relationships developed by the board and the commissioner through informal briefings for legislators held during the year. These get-togethers have been perceived as successful by other state agencies, which have now moved to imitate the regents in legislative relationships.

The Legislature

Legislators were generally aware of the need to solve the crisis in aid to education if they were to proceed with the passage of a budget. Our survey shows that legislators' opinions about solutions were divided, with approximately one-third favoring an increase (and the necessary taxes), one-third calling for greater economy, and one-third supporting formula changes. A few just wanted to see that their home areas "got their share." Most, however, seemed to be waiting the leadership to break the logjam. "Education will do alright," said one assemblyman. "Education is seen as being of special importance by both the speaker and minority leader."

The central problem was the budget. For Republicans this was a party measure and they would do little until the leadership gave them the cue. They had heard from their constituents, whose sentiment was in favor of increased school aid by almost two-to-one, according to the survey results. These legislators, however, could not identify the other areas of state activity their people would like to see cut. Welfare was a likely target, as it was in 1968, but beyond than that few legislators could suggest further reductions without the risk of offending some groups back home.

The Democrats had a different problem with the budget. They opposed not only the cuts in education but also the cuts in welfare and other activities that served the populations of the cities. In addition, they wanted to substitute a more sharply progressive income tax for the sales tax proposal of the governor. The minority party had some hope that conservative Republicans in the assembly might join them to defeat the sales tax. The Democrats realized, however, that the leadership would seek compromises to hold on to these votes when the budget was finally presented.

The chairman of the JLC continued to work behind the scenes, presenting his case for retaining $760 and defeating the formula changes. His staff supplied information to legislators about the effects on school districts in their bailiwicks. It was pointed out to the assembly speaker how districts in his suburban Long Island area would suffer reductions amounting to over $8 million.

Decisions by the Leadership

The assembly remained the critical arena. Could the governor's budget be passed if the cuts in education remained? If not, would holding to the $760 ceiling be a sufficient palliative to insure passage of the sales tax? With all 72 Democrats opposed to the tax, the 11 Conservative-Republicans among the majority's 78 members held the key votes. Spending cuts had to be made or these 11 would not support the tax. If education were cut too deeply, however, other Republicans might vote with the Democrats to defeat the budget.

Speaker Duryea and Majority Leader Brydges met during the third week in March to review the entire budget problem. They decided that education was the critical item in the budget. The full measure of cuts was a risky course to take. No solution was reached on how to proceed, but the outlines of a compromise were developed. The central idea was to retain the ceiling at $760 per-pupil, according to a member of the Republican leadership.

The following Monday the two leaders met with Governor Rockefeller. The education matter was settled by continuing the $760 ceiling, reducing the state share from 49 to 46 percent, but delaying its effect until 1970, and allocating approximately $52 million in urban aid through the end of 1969. Because these compromises reflected many of Senator Dominick's proposals Brydges called on him to draft the bills. These were introduced a few days later and Dominick led the debate in the senate.

The budget and sales tax passed easily in the senate by a strict party vote of 33-to-24 on each measure. In the assembly the two bills went through easily when two upstate Democratic assemblymen crossed the aisle to vote with the Republicans. The budget passed by 77-to-72 and the tax increase by 78-to-70.*

---

*Both defecting assemblymen were censured by the Democratic caucus. One retired and was appointed to the State Civil Service

Aftermath

A major step in New York State education was made during the 1969 session—the creation of a State Commission on the Quality, Cost and Financing of Elementary and Secondary Education. Rockefeller suggested the commission is his annual message, but the legislature did not act on it until March after the compromises for school aid in the coming year had been reached.[7] It was another seven months before the governor appointed Manly Fleischmann, a Buffalo attorney, as chairman of the commission.

The purpose of the Fleischmann Commission was to investigate all aspects of the public schools' objectives, programs, expenditures, and administration. It was to make recommendations as it saw fit regarding state and local financing, administrative arrangements, teacher employment and compensation agreements, teacher performance, and any other conditions that the commission believed had an effect on school quality and costs.

The first report of the commission was to be made in 1971, hopefully in time for consideration by the 1972 legislature. There were delays, however, and the commission staff was not brought together until January 1970. Its initial report was not made to the governor and the legislature until January 1972.

During the next two legislative sessions the struggle over the aid ceiling followed much the same pattern as in 1969. The 1970 session raised the ceiling to $860 and restored state sharing to 49 percent. In 1971 there was no change made in these policies due, in part, to the impending report of the Fleischmann Commission.

The first volume of the commission report contained radical proposals for changing the educational finance structure. The announcement of them in January 1972 sent shock waves through the legislature. The commission recommended complete state financing of elementary and secondary schools on a per-pupil basis. The property tax was to be collected by the state for an interim period of 10 years while other state revenues would gradually be shifted to education support. Equal educational opportunity was to be provided by equal per-pupil financing in all districts. The commission requested that $715 million be added to the governor's $2.3 billion school aid request for 1972-73 to begin the changeover.[8]

The governor did not request action on the report and the legislature simply chose to ignore the commission's proposals during the 1972 session. The commission's goals seemed politically unreal

---

Commission by Governor Rockefeller. The other became a Republican and was returned to the assembly from the same district in 1970.

to some, too idealistic to become a program on which politicians could act. According to others, however, the recommendations will eventually have to be implemented if the state's education system is to remain viable.[9]

The strategies and processes in school aid policy-making observed in the 1969 session are not unusual for New York State. The governor proposes a program and a budget to which all others in the process react. His central purpose is to obtain passage of this budget. Given a legislative majority of his own party, he can usually expect a minimum of difficulty. At the outset the governor can accept or reject the recommendations of the regents as suits his purposes without fear of any differences between them becoming a rallying point for opposition in the legislature. His next task is to meet any counterdemands in the legislature by the opposition party, dissidents in his own party, or the educational interest groups. The governor's strategy is one of letting the legislative leadership gauge the pressures and advise him on necessary modifications. At the same time, however, the legislative leadership realizes that modifications leading to additional taxes or offending a large proportion of the electorate will be blamed on the legislature.

DECENTRALIZATION OF NEW YORK CITY SCHOOLS

School redistricting policy is the responsibility of the legislature, although the development and conduct of such policies has usually been given over to the regents. City school systems were created in 1917 by the legislature on the advice of the regents. Separate districts in each city were consolidated under a single board of education responsible for the operation and management of the schools. The objective was to achieve greater efficiency and economy. The reduction of political influence in school government was also an objective. The Home Rule for Cities Act eliminated 250 laws pertaining to school districts in cities—laws that could be changed only by legislative action.[10] Provision was also made for school-community boards to advise the central board on local school matters. These groups were rarely used and the central boards alone came to determine local policies.

Discussion of decentralizing city schools by transferring limited authority from a central board to local school-community boards began in New York about 1964. The impetus came from community groups, particularly minorities, seeking a voice in determining educational goals, school programs, and how funds are spent. Questions of racial integration and separatism have been part of the discussion. More important, questions about the division of political control of the schools and the regulation of expenditures, employment, and supervision have been part of the debate. New York City, the focus of discussion, is the only city school system in the state that has been decentralized.

Background to 1969

There were three main threads in the struggle over decentralization of New York City schools: the thrust of blacks toward community control, the determination of the UFT to hold on to its power to bargain with the Board of Education on a city-wide basis, and the apparent inability of city officials to find a solution to these problems while retaining overall authority for school policy-making. As the three threads became more entangled state officials were called upon to attempt to aid the several sides in settling the matter. Lack of progress by the City Board of Education and hardening of union and minority group positions after each of these attempts eventually resulted in a legislative denouement.

Between 1954 and 1961 black organizations and their white liberal allies in the New York City watched with increasing dismay the inept attempts of the Board of Education to reduce racial segregation in the schools. Steps in this direction, such as changes in attendance areas and freedom of transfer, seemed halting and confused. In the hope of helping to find a solution, the 1961 legislature required the board to revitalize local school advisory boards and take the opinions of community groups into consideration when providing for neighborhood schools. Most board efforts in this direction, however, did not get beyond the planning stage and segregation increased with changing neighborhood patterns.[11]

The UFT was drawn into the situation after it won the right to be the sole bargaining agent for the city's nearly 50,000 teachers following a 1961 teachers' strike. The union then sought greater job security and increased rights in the rules governing teacher supervision, promotion, and transfer. These changes would reduce the powers of principals and supervisors relative to the powers of teachers. The changes would also reduce the flexibility of the board in devising arrangements for decentralization and bring the UFT into direct conflict with community groups as decentralization became more of an issue.

State education officials began to play a continuing role in 1963. The City Board of Education had relied on voluntary open enrollment since 1961 to curb school segregation. Civil rights leaders became convinced that this would fail and called on the board to present a timetable for desegregation. When this was not done the civil rights groups called for a boycott of the schools and nearly half of the City's pupils stayed home one day. The board then turned to Commissioner Allen and asked him to make a study of the schools and develop specific plans for desegregation. Allen's response was to form an Advisory Committee on Human Relations and Community Tensions. When the committee reported in 1964 its key recommendation for beginning desegregation was to replace junior high schools with integrated middle schools.[12] The board made plans to implement this recommendation through the creation of 31 local districts but was unable to rally sufficent support; the plans were not carried out.

By 1965 protesting blacks were turning away from integration and toward community control as a means of obtaining school program improvements. If the pattern of segregation could not be broken then blacks would seek teachers and curricula appropriate for all-black schools. The board turned in this direction in 1967, but quite by accident.

Mayor John Lindsay asked the state for more money for city schools based on the fact that each of New York City's five boroughs are legally defined as counties. The legislature's response, pressed by upstate Republicans, was that to qualify for the aid requested each county, or city borough, would have to become a separate school district. Lindsay appointed a panel headed by Ford Foundation President McGeorge Bundy to prepare proposals for decentralization. Meanwhile, the board, aided by Ford money, established three experimental districts for decentralization and local board operation. They were the I.S. 201 complex, Two Bridges, and Ocean Hill-Brownsville districts.

The Ocean Hill-Brownsville experiment led to the final drawing of the battle lines. The local district's teachers, with UFT support, participated in the community planning group for the district. The plan was made and executed more quickly than the teachers expected and they were not consulted as they thought they would be. The Board of Education received the plan and, before it could react, a local governing board had been elected and proceeded to select school principals. The teachers refused to participate, but the City Board appointed four of the five men recommended by the local board.

Shortly thereafter the UFT struck the city system for higher wages and improved educational services. Although the strike call was unrelated to the experimental district problem, the Ocean Hill governing board took it as an affront to their selection of principals and brought in parents to teach during the walkout. The board also claimed the right to evaluate, transfer, and dismiss teachers as it saw fit. This was a direct attack on the rights of teachers gained by bargaining with the City Board, according to the UFT.

In the spring of 1968 the governing board in Ocean Hill dismissed 19 teachers. The City Board declared this action illegal but failed to change the position taken by the Ocean Hill board. The Union struck the entire system to protest both the local district's action and the City Board's failure to live up to its contract. Attempts at arbitration were unsuccessful and the state had to take over the administration of Ocean Hill-Brownsville.

This situation clearly demarked the positions of the union and the community groups. The union would henceforth examine decentralization almost strictly from the point of view of contract enforcement and city-wide uniformity in personnel practices. The community groups would press for greater autonomy in hiring and evaluating teachers in local districts. All of these factors would figure prominently in the legislative considerations to follow.

In this environment the Bundy panel finally completed a plan to solve the problem and it was submitted to the 1968 legislature. It called for 30 to 60 legally autonomous districts with local governing boards to establish curricula and to hire and assign personnel in accordance with state requirements. A central board would continue to operate the high schools but its main function would be long-range planning.[13] The Bundy plan became the basis for several other plans, including Mayor Lindsay's, which would have retained greater power over school operation in the hands of the central board, and the regents' modifications, which would have established 15 districts, with the central board retaining authority over interdistrict teacher transfers but leaving intradistrict personnel matters in the hands of local boards acting under state requirements.

All three of these plans were rejected by the 1968 legislature. The Bundy plan was rejected because it did not have the regents' endorsement. The regents' plan was rejected because it came too late in the session. The mayor's plan was rejected because, like the Bundy plan, it was opposed by the UFT. The Ocean Hill situation also played a part; legislators did not want to act until the union and the city settled their contractual differences. Acting earlier might have been viewed as legislative interference in a local labor dispute.

The pressure for community control in New York City, as evidenced in the Ocean Hill situation, was strong. Thus the 1968 legislature reached a compromise, passing a bill sponsored by Senator John Marchi, Republican from Staten Island, one of New York City's boroughs. The Marchi bill directed the City Board of Education to prepare a plan for development of a community school system to be submitted to the regents and the legislature by December 1968,[14] thus placing the entire problem in the hands of the legislature in the next session.

When the legislature met in January 1969 the major question was just how far it would go in using state powers to settle a local problem. The question was particularly sensitive, given the fact that any solution would have to be voted by a Republican majority drawn largely from upstate constituencies, whereas downstate New York City was represented largely by Democrats. In addition, there was little hope of finding a consensus among the New York City delegation as it contained reform, liberal, and regular Democrats, and some conservative Republicans. The controversy was exacerbated by divisions between black and white legislators; and strong pro-labor factions among the regular Democrats. Among upstate Republicans, on the other hand, there would be little support for any plan not endorsed by the regents, for these legislators have traditionally looked to the educational government for solutions to redistricting problems.

At the outset the legislative leadership and Governor Rockefeller agreed that any solution must have the backing of the majority of New York City Democrats in the legislature. Rockefeller also let it be known, according to an education department official, that he would support the regents in their efforts to solve the problem. If it had to be solved at the state level he wanted it solved with the endorsement of the state's educational government above partisan politics insofar as possible. This, the governor believed, would lessen the appearance of a politically imposed solution.

Thus the roles of the major actors were clear at the outset. The governor and the legislative leadership looked to the minority party, particularly legislators from New York City, to make the choices on decentralization proposals. There was one proviso. The governor wanted these choices to be ones endorsed by the regents and thus carry educational rather than political overtones. Most of the Republican majority could then be convinced to vote for the measure. The regents wanted a solution to New York City's problem that would give sufficient power to each of the competing forces. The Democrats, however, were factionally divided and acting under differing pressures by their constituencies and interest groups, including the labor unions in New York City. While the legislative battle would be centered on a series of proposals, the critical question was how much political wrangling the governor and the legislative leaders could tolerate before a solution was achieved.

The 1969 Session

Two plans were placed before the 1969 legislature. The plan of the City Board, based on the Bundy Report, provided for community

119

boards elected in 30 districts with the power to hire and transfer teachers within the districts. The boards could also determine curricula within state regulations and administer funds after the City Board approved their budgets. The City Board was to be made up of 13 members appointed by the mayor.

The regents' proposal was a modification of this plan and called for a range of 20 to 30 districts, grievance procedures for teacher transfer problems, and authorization for districts to establish their budgets within a lump sum allocation from the City Board. The board was to be replaced by a five-member salaried central authority.[15]

The City Board bill was quickly dropped because it did not have the regents' endorsement. It was unacceptable to the UFT because it included extensive community control. This effectively took the City Board out of the situation and left it to the legislature to offer counterproposals to the regents' measure.

The first compromise was a bill by Senator Marchi that would reduce the emphasis on community control by restricting local district autonomy in personnel and finance matters. It was designed to appeal to the UFT and, as it moved toward the regents' plan, to upstate legislators. As might be expected, however, the Marchi bill did not appeal either to black interest groups or to liberal Democrats. The UFT refused to support the bill because it felt that it still gave local districts too much, too soon. The union wanted more time to find ways of dealing with the new centers of power that would emerge. This ended any possible support by the regular Democrats, who feared such support would offend labor.

A liberal Democrat, Assemblyman Jerome Kretchmer of New York City, then began rallying Democrats to support the regents' bill. He argued that Democratic legislators could not vote for the Marchi measure and still face constituents who wanted local control. But a vote for the regents' bill carried the risk of making an enemy of the UFT, so Kretchmer's effort soon faded, paving the way for further compromise.

Assembly Minority Leader Stanley Steingut, an influential New York City Democrat, lent his support to an effort to solve the racial and union problems first and then make the decentralization plan. The proposal was developed, issue by issue, to steer a course between militants and conservatives on community control. Several black Democrats participated in these discussions. Safeguards for the UFT were developed in consultation with Albert Shanker, president of the union. According to The New York Times, these discussions were secret to avoid any accusations that either the black community or the union was "selling out" to the other on community control. Premature disclosure of these negotiations by a legislator in a television interview led to their breakdown because Shanker felt it necessary to withdraw.[16]

Steingut persisted. He knew that all factions of the New York City Democratic party had to be involved in a solution. He retrieved the situation by bringing in Albert Blumenthal, the deputy minority leader and a leader of the reform Democrats. This salvaged the situation and a successful compromise offering reduced community control and gaining at least tacit union support through the Steingut safeguards seemed imminent.

Kretchmer and several black legislators, however, opposed this compromise and sought support for the regents' bill. Regent Kenneth Clark, a black, also opposed the compromise and obtained the private agreement of the regents to repudiate it. When it came to a vote the several black legislators came out against the Steingut bill. Word of the regents' repudiation turned upstate Republicans against it and the UFT disavowal curtailed Democratic support.[17] The bill was defeated.

After this compromise failed the decentralization effort collapsed and the actors dissolved again into separate camps. Shanker endorsed the dormant Marchi bill, knowing full well it could not gain sufficent support, thus essentially saying that the union would prefer no bill at all in 1969. On the other hand, black legislators could not back out and still face their constituents, nor could the liberal and reform Democrats.

Governor Rockefeller was faced with a critical decision. Should he let the issue slip back out of the legislature and add further chaos to the New York City school situation or should he use Republican votes and get a bill? A conference of about 12 black and Puerto Rican legislators convinced the Republican leadership that no bill meant chaos. These legislators proposed themselves as the nucleus of a compromise. This convinced the governor of the need for a bill for the sake not only of the city but of his own political stature, according to an education department official. Calling in the Republican leadership, he told them that all deals were off. "We've heard from everybody," he said. "Now we're going to write the bill." In doing so he committed Republican votes to solving the issue, but a strategy still had to be devised.

The regents' bill was used as a starting point. This would add upstate Republican strength to the black and Puerto Rican bloc. In addition, the elements of community control in the regents' bill would bring in some liberal Democrats. There would be a loss of other liberal and reform Democrats who wanted greater community control, however, thus jeopardizing the governor's prospects of pleasing a substantial portion of the New York City delegation. The bill also precluded support from the union, which wanted less community control.

The leadership worked out the compromises in close cooperation with the regents, the blacks, and the Puerto Ricans. Upstate Republicans were asked for their views. Steingut was consulted and portions of his measure were incorporated in the drafting of the bill, particularly those items that preserved the union's bargaining position with the New York City Board. The governor and his staff then held separate conferences with the blacks and their supporters. The final bill was drafted by a counsel to the senate majority leader.

Before the bill went to the floor 10 Republican assemblymen from New York City voiced opposition to it. They were conservative Republicans who wanted an elected central school board with most of the board's current powers retained. Another round of conferences was held by the governor and the legislative leaders, first with black and Puerto Rican legislators, then with New York City Republicans. The task was to avoid using upstate Republican votes to impose a solution on City Republicans, an undesirable move in a closely divided lower house. After several concessions were made the governor stopped all talks and the bill was sent to the floor.[18] He let it be known among Republican lawmakers that this was the bill to be passed. He also threatened to call a special legislative session on decentralization if it were not approved, a move that would focus attention on the legislature's attempts at solution rather than on the governor's role. On the floor the bill received passionate support from black assemblymen, the senate majority leader, and some City Democrats. The bill passed the senate by a vote of 48-to-9 and the assembly by 125-to-23.

Aftermath

The decentralization bill was characterized as workable by a City Board of Education official. The measure provided for 30-to-33 semiautonomous districts, each with a locally elected governing board. Teachers would be selected by the local board from a qualifying list but subject to the union-board contract for interdistrict transfer. The board would control expenditures after its budget had been approved by the Central Board. The governor sweetened the financial pie by adding a $250,000 maintenance fund for each district to spend without reference to the Central Board. The Central Board was to have seven members, one to be appointed by each of the five borough presidents and two by the mayor. The chief administrative officer would be designated "chancellor" and chosen by the board. The bill has provided a basis on which to begin the decentralization process. Several adjustments were made in 1971 with regard to principals' appointments but decentralization has proceeded.

CONCLUSIONS FROM THE CASES

The legislative process is a system of constantly changing interrelationships among the several actors. The characteristics of these interrelationships are tied to the variety of role behavior available to the actors. Which behaviors they take on is determined by basic role expectations, ideologies, available strategies, relative power, and risks involved in the situation. Ultimately each actor must reconcile his behavior with his supporters, both in and outside of the policy system, and with their expectations of authoritative action resulting in outputs.

In both cases the governor figured prominently as a proposer and a decider of what was to be done. His power to control a legislative majority of his own party and his ability to put the onus of higher taxes or a failure to reach solutions on the legislature gave him tremendous leverage in both situations. Essentially legislators were forced to seek compromises that were acceptable to the governor rather than to the legislative factions.

Legislative leaders had the task of determining what compromises to present to the governor. Up to a point majority members could be held in line. As pressures for alternative solutions by educational interest groups and constituents increased, however, the leaders had to decide the courses to propose that would satisfy the legislators as well as the governor. In these decisions the leaders also had to make judgments about the minority position, particularly in the closely divided assembly.

Individual legislators on both sides of the aisle played a variety of roles. Some became internal lobbyists for particular points of view, while others sought compromises to be offered to the leadership. In the end, however, legislators had to accept the concessions granted by the governor at the point when he decided that action would be taken. In the face of strict party discipline imposed by the leaders there were no alternative choices left.

The Board of Regents played a part in both situations. But the role it played was controlled by the governor through his strategy of using only those parts of the board's proposals that reenforced his position. The board had some influence on legislators, but was limited to the extent that the governor permitted it to become a center of alternative proposals or advisory opinions.

The interest groups' impact was different in each case. The upstate groups acted directly on the legislature on the level of finance by lobbying to bring about a compromise. In decentralization the New York City interest groups operated almost entirely through their individual legislators. Their representatives were available to the leadership and the governor and were called in at critical points.

8

This final chapter offers a summary and theoretical exploration of the interactions of the actor groups involved in the educational policy-making process. The findings of the study will be summarized and a systems approach to the policy-making process, evolved out of the understanding established, will be described. Out of this conceptualization an attempt to explore the future of the policy-making system in New York will be made. Finally, thoughts on the problems and possibilities of policy-making analysis at the state level will be presented.

PURPOSE, PROCESS, AND FINDINGS

The purpose of the book has been to describe the actors and their interrelations in the policy-making process of education in New York State. The central actor group was perceived to be the state legislature. The legislative arena is that in which accommodations are ultimately made as policies are established. The governor, the regents and the State Education Department, the educational interest groups, and individual legislators were portrayed as actors who participate in the policy process.

Several methods were employed. First, document search led to the identification of actors in educational policy-making at the state level. Second, unstructured interviews with people identified through documents were carried out to clarify further the ways in which the policy-making system works, particularly as it pertains to education. Next, structured interviews were held with interest group leaders to establish their perceptions of the policy-making process. Finally, an in-depth survey instrument was administered to members of the state legislature. The instrument was adapted from Wahlke, et al.[1] The purpose of the instrument was to ascertain legislators' policy-making behavior, particularly in relationship with other actors. The instrument was centered on the dynamics of interactions among the actors involved in the policy-making process.

Extensive field work was carried out during the 1969 legislative session. At that time attempts were made to establish an accurate perception of the interactions among actors involved in the process; legislators, the governor, the regents and the State Education Department, and educational interest groups. Three succeeding legislative sessions were observed to ascertain the effects of the policies that resulted from the interactions of actor groups during the 1969 legislative session.

The findings described and explained in Chapters 3 through 6 focused on the four main actor groups. To set the stage for the conceptual model of interaction in the policy-making system, it is useful first to summarize the major findings derived about each actor group.

The State Legislature

The general theme was to depict the state legislature as a processing system. To maintain that processing system there are several subsystems. Specifically, there are the parties,* the formal leadership, and the committee system. Cutting across these subsystems is the flow of information, which provides the knowledge by which they carry out their tasks. Party politics, although not as blatant as in the past, is still an important element in the legislature's processing system. Control of the legislature, particularly in the assembly, has long been closely contested by the Republicans and the Democrats, requiring party leaders to maintain relatively tight party discipline. The legislative leadership is chosen by the majority party and wields much power, controlling committee assignments, legislative staffing, and the flow of bills. The leadership committees, the rules committees in both houses as well as the

---

*A less formal subsystem than party, but nevertheless very real and important, is the differentiation of legislators along ideological lines. These include urban-suburban-rural splits as well as conservative vs. liberal views of the role of the state in supporting such social services as welfare, health, and education. These variations often tend to blur party distinctions when ideological policy considerations are being debated and voted on.

Finance Committee in the senate and the Ways and Means Committee in the assembly, dominate policy proposals. The extent to which bills go to substantive committees is based upon the confidence of the majority leader or speaker in the chairmen of the particular committees. This exercise of power by the leadership is in conformity with the norms of the system. That is, legislators know and abide by "the rules of the game," which assure the maintenance of the system. These rules appear to vary somewhat between the contentious, but disciplined asesmbly and the club-like, polycentric senate, but, in the final analysis, party and leadership play dominant and accepted roles in the legislature.

Supporting the processing activities of the legislature is information, which is required to make decisions. Internal sources of information, somewhat insufficient in the past, have been improved since the late 1960s and should provide legislators with even more reliable information in the future. There have already been dramatic improvements. The New York State legislature was ranked first among the 50 state legislatures as being well-informed in a 1970 survey.[2] This has implications for the traditional external information providers, especially educational interest groups that hope to influence the legislature through provision of information. In short, the legislature might be moving to free itself of dependency on external sources of information.

Of particular interest was the way the legislature processes educational policy. The point was made that legislators are impressively knowledgeable about educational issues. Many noted as "experts" by their colleagues focus much of their legislative attention on this area. Both perceptual and behavioral evidence indicates that educational policy-making is treated much the same as any other substantive policy area in the legislature. As sources of influence about educational policy acknowledged experts in the legislature and the views of "the people back home" are most relevant to legislators as they decide how to vote on educational measures. Views of party leaders and executive department agencies are reported to be least influential. One other source of influence, the state commissions on education, which tend to convene about once a decade, have a potential for moving the legislature toward adopting major modifications in programmatic emphases and in state aid patterns.

The Governor

The governor of the state of New York commands broad powers that place him in a dominant policy-proposing position. These powers include party leadership, responsibility to establish an executive budget, veto and line-item veto, and broad patronage prerogatives. Such powers assure the governor a central legislative role. In the 1940s Governor Dewey employed these powers fully, setting a precedent for governors who followed. The major factors that affect the ability of the governor to bring these powers to bear are:

1. The governor's party and the majority party in the legislature. When the two are of the same party political control is usually more easily applied in achieving the governor's program.

2. The special needs of New York City. Any governor must take New York City's needs into account or risk loss of votes in the legislature and possibly at the polls.

3. The thrust of the governor's program. The governor's program must provide for long-range state-wide needs, not merely "something for everyone," if he hopes to have the legislature rally behind it.

The governor can step in as an actor in the educational policy-making process when he so desires, but prefers to remain in the background if at all possible. Although the Board of Regents, as the agency constitutionally responsible for education, takes the lead in education in New York State, the governor through his many devices remains an important actor in the process. He has relative freedom of choice to pick the issues with which he wishes to become involved. This arrangement enables him to avoid political difficulties that accompany proposed changes in educational policy.

The governor has support arms that monitor movement of major legislative proposals in education and closely observe the activities of the regents and the State Education Department. The Division of the Budget researches all state agencies' funding requests and contrasts these with expected state revenues. Because the division also prepares the governor's budget it maintains constant communication with executive agencies, including the State Education Department, which attempts, in turn, to maintain maximum independence of the governor's budget-makers. The Office of Planning Coordination, part of the Office of Planning Services since 1971, reviews the agencies' activities and goals in an effort to maintain a unified thrust toward major government goals. Because of the regents' relative independence the Office of Planning Coordination and the Division of the Budget usually find themselves reviewing regents' proposals after they have already been made public. The governor's program staff (i.e., the counsels, assistant counsels, program associates, and the secretary to the governor) is concerned with political ramifications of both the governor's program and other proposals that wend their way through the legislature. This staff advises the governor on potential political effects of his signing or not signing specific bills into law. To do this his program staff maintains constant communications with executive agencies, the legislature, and many interest groups.

The Board of Regents
and the State Education Department

The Board of Regents, often referred to as a "fourth branch of government," is relatively independent of the governor's office. This independence derives from several factors, including the executive, legislative, and judicial powers granted the regents by the state constitution and subsequent statutory enactments, the fifteen year terms of office of each of the regents' fifteen members, and the ability of the regents' administrative arm, the State Education Department, to monitor the state's educational scene and make well-documented recommendations to the regents.

The regents have moved into a more political role in the policy-making arena. Controversial issues such as bussing, redistricting, curricular reforms, taxation, and employment conditions of teachers have all required the regents to play a more interactive role. Indications of this movement include the Board of Regents' willingness to take a public stand in favor of increased state taxes to support its requests for funding of educational programs and the development of a legislative program that is distributed to the governor, the legislature, and the public. The regents' policy-making involvement begins with studies either commissioned to outside sources or assigned to the State Education Department. When data and discussions result in agreement the board establishes educational goals and policy thrusts. The department is assigned the task of carrying out these goals and policies where authority is clearly established or preparing legislative bills when new laws are required.

The chief administrative officer of the State Education Department, the commissioner of education, is selected by the regents; the governor selects all but 3 of the 21 executive agency heads. The commissioner's duties include advising the Board of Regents and carrying out regents' policies. He is supported by executive, deputy, associate, and assistant commissioners, as well as by bureau heads and more than 3,000 agency employees.

The regents' legislative program is derived from an identifiable process. Initially suggestions that come from the regents, the department, the interest groups, or individual legislators are screened by the legal arm of the department to ascertain their legal feasibility. Those that survive this test are reviewed in the commissioner's office to see if they are consonant with the board's goals and policies, then consolidated into a package. Draft bills are drawn up and the commissioner and regents make the final decision on which measures to recommend. The program is then distributed and the department's top officials set out to convince the governor and the legislature that major requests should be approved. Where possible the governor is asked to incorporate these requests in his own legislative program.

Legislators view the regents as political amateurs but useful to their own political needs. They feel that regents' proposals such as racial integration of schools are politically naive. If the regents had to stand for election, legislators believe, they would not make such proposals. At the same time legislators find that the board is useful when it comes to taking the criticism concerning legislation such as that dealing with the consolidation of school districts. Historically relations between the educational interest groups and the Board of Regents have been amicable, with neither group capturing the other. The ECB and the regents have kept each other informed of activities being pursued and have joined together to influence policy-making when they have felt that there might be mutual benefit. The future, however, might be somewhat different. If educational interest groups realign as teacher militancy increases, relations between the regents and the interest groups will have to be redefined.

Educational Interest Groups

Criteria for selection of the interest groups analyzed included the anomic-nonassociational-institutional-associational continuum developed by Gabriel A. Almond and G. Bingham Powell,[3] and the Scope of Interest and Depth of Intervention model developed by Sayre and Kaufman.[4] On the basis of these frameworks six educational interest groups were selected for analysis. Iannaccone's typology of structural formats for educational interest groups at the state level was explored.[5] The present situation in New York State was presented in light of this typology.

Although New York's educational interest groups are characterized as cooperative, e.g., in sharing data and lobbying jointly for increases in state aid, it is likely that these groups in the future will compete for favored treatment by formal government role-players. The present coalition of interest groups in the state is tenuous. This is due in part to the fact that the umbrella organization, the ECB, does not play a leadership role in meeting emerging educational problems. It is also related to mounting teacher militancy, which is best illustrated by the growing role of the UFT in New York City. This teachers' union movement has challenged the state teacher's professional organization (NYSTA) to become more militant and play an adversary role with school board and administrative organizations. In 1972 members of NYSTA and the UFT's state counterpart, the United Teachers of New York, set an historic precedent by voting to become the first united union and professional state teachers' organization in the country. The new joint organization is known as the New York State United Teachers. The impact of this recent merger is yet to be felt, but will probably be profound on the relationships among the interest groups and the relationships between the interest groups and other actors in the policy-making process.

The influencing mechanisms at the disposal of the educational interest groups include control over information that can be used by legislators and the governor in the policy-making process, the expertise ascribed to educators by lay citizens and government officials alike, the importance of children as a political "weapon", and the power of the vote held by members of the organizations and their friends.

Finally, how educational interest group leaders go about influencing legislators and the governor was explored and the views of legislators concerning the effectiveness of these procedures were contrasted to the interest groups' strategies. Whereas interest group leaders viewed the governor as the most critical access point in the policy-making process, legislators felt that the governor's role is not really that important. Interest group leaders viewed the legislature as highly centralized, while legislators felt that there is substantial room for individual legislator deviation from party and leadership control. Educational interest group leaders felt that their information inputs are vital to the legislative process, while legislators felt that this is but one of many possible information sources. Educational interest groups devoted much of their effort to state-level influencing, while legislators felt that the grass-roots influence of educators is more effective than that practiced by lobbyists in Albany. Several possible reasons for these perceptual variations include Eulau's notion of "strata"[6] and the changing complexion of the legislature in New York.

With the four major actor groups portrayed according to their perception of and behavior in the educational policy-making process, it is possible to move toward a conceptualization of that process. A systems framework will be developed to serve this purpose.

CONCEPTUALIZING THE POLICY-MAKING PROCESS:
A SYSTEMS FRAMEWORK

As noted, policy-making may be viewed as a cycle such as the Present-Preferred Cycle referred to in Chapter 1. This cycle is composed of six phases. A period of dissatisfaction by one or more groups in society, if great enough, can lead to a reformulation of attitudes that provides direction for action and also leads to the identification of leaders. Next, ideas are formulated that can be proposed as solutions to constraints. These are debated to widen the scope of involvement and clarify the concepts involved. When there has been discussion sufficient to raise the issue to a level of public awareness, the ideas are presented to the legislative bodies, which must make authoritative decisions. If ideas survive this process, they are then implemented as formal rules, regulations, or laws.

The focus of this study has been on the legislative phase of the cycle as the critical market place in which societal demands are processed, rejected, or accepted. This process, which is political in nature, can be usefully described as a system. As David Easton notes, "a political system can be designated as those interactions through which values are authoritatively allocated for society."[7] A systems framework permits a view of the connecting links in the New York State political, or policy-making system as factors related to inputs, thruputs, and outputs. Figure 3, a simplified visualization of this process as it might be applied to state policy-making, represents a basic processing system. Components include inputs (resources and demands), thruputs (processing activities), and outputs (system maintenance and products).

Input resources include acceptance by the environment of the policy system's legitimacy, fiscal support, and human energy. All three resource bases must be secured to maintain the system. There must be initial legitimization, (i.e., basic agreement in the form of a constitution or charter), willingness of citizens to support public services, and desire on the part of qualified people to participate in the policy-making system. The extent to which these resource inputs are available sets the initial limits of the policy-making system's ability to process its tasks.

Input demands initiate activities in the policy-making system. As noted in the Present-Preferred Cycle, these input demands usually start as societal dissatisfactions. Those that persist long enough to attract wide support crystallize around alternatives that are presented to legislative bodies. For example, the indignation of blacks and many whites eventually led to civil rights and school integration recommendations that are being processed by legislative bodies at all levels of the federal system.

Thruput processes encompass formal legislative bodies as well as other groups whose roles in the policy-making process influence deliberations and outputs. These activities are carried on within an authority structure in which roles and communication networks among

FIGURE 3

The Policy-Making System

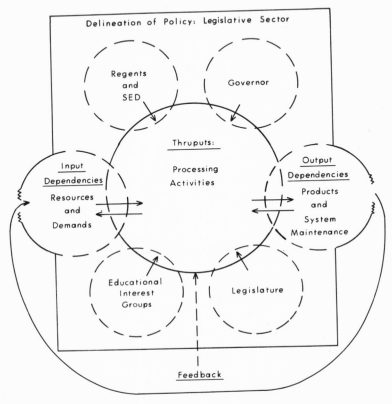

role players are fairly well-defined. Influence mechanisms employed range from threat of reprisal to promise of reward. Influencing by threats and promises includes delivering or withholding votes, providing or withholding resources such as information, offering or withholding support for appointment to prestigious positions, and promising tradeoffs of support for policy proposals.

Outputs include products and system maintenance. Products are usually packaged in the form of legislation and are executed by administrative agencies. System maintenance is the effort given over to the morale and satisfaction of the actor groups. This effort, in turn, assures the thruput sector of its continued existence. When processing inputs the thruput sector must be concerned that it does not consume human resources to such an extent that it will be unable to react to further input demands. Thus extensive efforts are made to maintain effective working relationships among legislators and between legislators and other groups.

Finally, feedback is necessary to gauge future courses of action. Members of the input sector review policy products for appropriateness and the resources they can be expected to consume. If there is much dissatisfaction with these products the input sector will probably raise the level of its demands and/or reduce its resource inputs to the thruput sector. Because of these possibilities the thruput sector tries to obtain preliminary feedback on the potential effects its products will have on the input sector. That is, it tries to reduce the risk of rejection and increase the potential for acceptance of policy products. For example, such phenomena as legislators visiting with their constituents or sending them opinion polls are aimed at getting such before-the-fact-feedback.

The thruput sector processes its tasks within an environmental context. As one of the authors has previously noted, to process its tasks adequately and assure its own maintenance "it must comprehend and isolate that which is its relevant and direct environment, learn to interact successfully with it and adapt its own systematic processes to the mutual acceptance of the environment and the system itself."[8] The environment is composed of the entire state, although some would argue that it includes the entire nation. It is in this amorphous environment that conditions under which the system functions are initially developed. For example, citizens' demands for control of their schools in New York City is one potent reminder of the constraining nature of the environment. Controversies over bussing students to achieve racial integration and ever-mounting taxes are further examples of mitigating variables that affect the thruput sector's willingness and ability to provide resources for public education.

This general systems framework can help place the activities and interrelations of actor groups in the policy-making process in perspective. The case of New York State can be used as an example of how this system might exist in other states. The reader will have to make appropriate modifications in transferring these concepts to other states, however, because the allocation of outputs in the several states is the result of "the intricate interplay of particular ideologies, individuals, institutions, and interest groups."[9]

A Caution

Before placing the actor groups studied into the framework of a system it might be well to pause for a moment and state necessary reservation. A systems approach might be useful in placing conceptual "hangers" on the findings of a study such as the present one, but the systems approach has not yet proven itself able to guide the collection of data. The concept of systems used here is strictly in this latter mode, i.e., to help explain what was found. No claim is made that it provided the general framework for data collection. The writers agree with Gerald Sroufe, who notes that while system approaches are more window dressing than actual fact as a methodological base for policy studies in education such approaches can "suggest the larger canvas, the total picture of which one's study is but a piece."[10]

INTERACTION OF THE ROLE-PLAYERS
IN THE POLICY-MAKING SYSTEM

For the purpose of description the systems framework concept can be very helpful. Regarding the present study the four actor groups can be described as playing roles in the policy-making process in a way that depicts dynamic interplay. As noted earlier, activities of these groups take place within the thruput sector of the input-thruput-output system framework. It is in this sector that authoritative allocations of values are assigned. Such allocations are the result of the interface of two variables—the actor groups and the institutional structures established for the purpose of deriving policy (see Figure 4). The actors have needs and desires, role orientations, and group affiliations that affect their participation. The structures' control systems, reward systems, and authority systems, set parameters for actor group interrelations.

The Actor Groups

The actors come to the process with predispositions, expectations, and orientations that are dependent upon their constituencies. Educational interest groups represent specialized memberships and attempt to maximize outcomes that favor these memberships. The Board of Regents and the State Education Department represent the entire educational system in the state and thus attempt to balance requests in their legislative program. The governor can have as much impact on the process as he wishes because he is the top elected official in the state and has significant powers that go with his position. The legislature's constituency, like the governor's, is the entire state, but this is complicated by the fact that legislators have varying perceptions, depending upon such factors as whether or not they are in the legislative leadership structure, how long they have served in the legislature, and which legislative districts they represent.

134

The actors also bring constraints to the process. The interest groups have no formal position in the process and therefore must devise effective strategies to impress government role players. The Board of Regents and the State Education Department are at the top of the educational hierarchy but at the bottom of the political hierarchy. To participate in the process they must consider political objectives as well as educational objectives. The governor seeks a balanced state budget and thus must weigh his support of education's needs very carefully. He can use the legislature and the Board of Regents to take much of the political criticism for increases in state aid, but the costs in the form of challenges to a balanced state budget can cause him to play a more active role. The legislature finds constraints in processing educational legislation because of ideological, geographical, constituent, and party differences. These constraints,

FIGURE 4

Dynamics of the Thruput Process

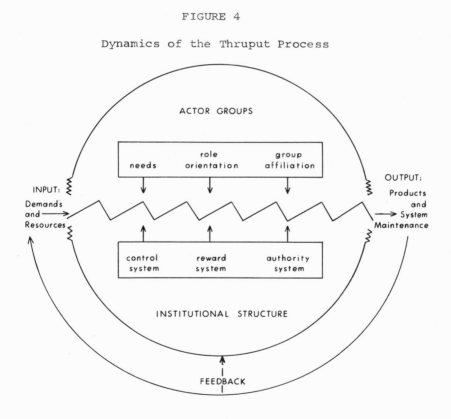

though not unique to educational issues, make it difficult at times for the legislature to process educational legislation.

The situation is complicated by the fact that role orientations of actors often cut across groups. For example, interest group leaders and legislative leaders tend to perceive the policy-making structure more similarly than do legislative leaders and the rank and file of the legislature. In a sense these two leadership groups have more in common than do the legislative leaders and other legislators. They mix frequently and tend to be around the capital for long tenures, so they know each other's objectives and strategies quite clearly. Similarly, the Board of Regents and State Education Department officials have relations of longer standing with the governor's key staff personnel (the secretary to the governor, for example, has been in state government service for 25 years) than they do with governors who, excepting Dewey and Rockefeller, have held office for only four or eight years.

The institutional structure, with its focal point in the legislature, exists as a vehicle for producing outputs that are demanded by environmental groups. It also exists to assure the maintenance of the thruput sector. To reduce risks of uncertainty of maintenance of the thruput sector and production of outputs the institutional structure is supported by rules and regulations that emanate from an authority system, a reward system, and a control system. These rules and regulations are often explicitly delineated in constitutional, statutory, and regulatory documents, but frequently they are only informally and implicitly agreed upon by members of the thruput sector. Thus legislators quickly learn the rules of the game and abuse them at their own peril. The governor is a critical factor in the policy-making process, but depends upon the legislative leadership to play active roles in building support for preferred policy alternatives. The Board of Regents is the apex educational governing body in the state and the interest groups are representatives of the several constituent members of the educational community. As such, although the Board of Regents and the interest groups often have common objectives they are limited in their ability and willingness to cooperate with each other, the governor, and the legislature in pursuing policy alternatives.

Because the actor groups must use the institutional structure to pursue their objectives and each has a legitimate role in that structure, they find themselves extensively interdependent upon each other. That is, the institutional structure for policy development includes rules and regulations that make it highly improbable that any one actor group can operate in total independence of the other actor groups.

Actor roles are being redefined, however, and, as a result, dependencies are undergoing modifications. Interest groups, for example, no longer seem to have a monopoly on information that legislators require to make intelligent decisions regarding educational policy. Instead the legislature is fast devising its own internal capacity to collect and interpret qualitative and quantitative data. The governor's office is also independently seeking to assess the education scene free of the interpretations of the interest groups, using, in particular, the Division of the Budget and the Office of Planning Services. In similar fashion, the increasing gap between the teacher groups and the administrator and board groups indicates that educational interest groups might become less cooperative in their interactions. Where in the past there have been common school support objectives toward which these groups worked cooperatively, there seem to be indications of intergroup competition to effect policy outcomes. Teachers have shown their organizational and political strength in collective negotiations in which administrators and board members are their adversaries. There are bound to be reverberations of these tense encounters in state-level interest group interactions. Related to this growing factionalism is the fact that the Educational Conference Board (ECB) continues to pursue a narrow program, reluctant to expand its interests to meet the emerging needs of urban education. As these needs find their way into the policy system it is probable that, unless the ECB changes its policy its influence will be diminished.

Both information control and teacher-administrator-board conflicts are indicators of changing relationships to come. As long as there remains a central authoritative policy center within government interdependence between actor groups will exist. The exact mix of that interdependence is impossible to forecast. The events of the late 1960s and early 1970s would indicate that the legislature and the governor will come to play more dominant roles and that the educational groups will be going through a long and difficult period of realignment, with many of their resources—human and fiscal—being funneled to the local school district level to support the internecine warfare between their member groups.

Even given all these unknowns, the authority hierarchy in the formal government sector of the thruput process appears to exhibit a remarkable continuity in format. Since the 1940s the governor has used his influence as the paramount state-wide elected official and leader of his party to retain the policy initiative. Within the legislature itself the leadership and the legislative experts tend to dominate the deliberations on major educational issues. Personalities might change and with them leadership styles (e.g., from Speaker Travia to Speaker Duryea), but the basic fact remains that the leaders retain

ultimate power and can dominate the legislative system if they so
desire. In short, the control process within the thruput sector is
based upon a tried and tested hierarchy of authority and power that
includes the governor and legislative leaders and is supported by a
complex set of rules and regulations to which the actors accepted as
having legitimate roles in the process must adhere.

In summary, actor groups interact with each other to deal with
demands made on the policy system by relevant environmental groups.
To meet these demands actor groups play out their roles within an
established institutional structure—a structure that has an identifiable
control structure, a reward system, and an authority system. The
thruput sector of the system is brought into action when institutional
and human variables come together. The institutional structure
provides the setting, but it is not sufficient; human variables interact
with it and leave their mark on the outputs produced in the structure.

THE STUDY OF STATE POLICY-MAKING

One of the greatest difficulties in attempting to transfer the
findings from a single state policy-making study to other states is
that there are such great differences among the states. There are
differences in relationships between the actor groups that result,
for example, from variations in constitutional restrictions on the
roles of legislators and governors and statutory regulations concerning
state education agencies, political traditions that persist over time,
idiosyncracies of various actor groups and their leaders, geographical locus, educational needs associated with the states' different
student population composition, the extent of responsibility for support
and control of public education assigned to the state, and the wealth
of the states.

To complicate the problem further, as Iannaccone notes,
"American educational policy-making patterns at the state level do
change."[11] In effect, even the findings concerning New York State
are only tentative in nature. As noted, there are significant indications
that the patterns of interactions among the actor groups that have
been established in the state appear to be undergoing stresses that
will lead to significant changes in future policy-making interrelationships. Thus there are dual policy-making problems in variations
from one state setting to another and policy-making changes over
time even within the context of a single state.

Once all this has been said, there still appear to be logical and
pressing reasons for attempting to systematize the study of state
educational policy-making to the point that it can become possible to
derive methodological and descriptive tools that can lead to general

statements about actor group interaction patterns. In the final analysis, as Frederick M. Wirt and Michael W. Kirst conclude, "all states are alike in being the object of increased political demands about school policies—curriculum, training of professionals, finances, and so on. All find expansion in their state school staffs, in their inter-actions with the local district, and in their involvement with federal programs."[12]

The several studies of the past decade that have attempted comparative analyses of state-level educational policy-making (e.g., Bailey, et al., 1962, Masters, et al., 1964, and Iannaccone, 1967)[13] have concluded that the differences between states are as prevalent as are their similarities. They further argue that given the present state of the art we are far from a level of conceputal knowledge that can serve as an adequate guide for future researchers to use as a basis for data gathering and analysis in state-level educational policy-making studies.

Viewing the situation from a more positive perspective, as insufficient as the base of substantive and conceptual knowledge might be, it is certainly well ahead of what it was before the studies noted above were carried out. These studies have also led to greatly expanded activities by researchers—both students of education and political scientists. Dissertations have been completed; courses in the politics of education have been established in universities, and research sponsored both by private foundations and by the federal government has been expanded. This activity has contributed to a growing literature base concerning educational policy making at the state level. Such studies, explorations, position papers, and hopefully the present case study can be used as a starting point for the develop-ment of the level of conceptual knowledge called for by the earlier studies.

State policy-making systems persist over time and thus afford the tenacious researcher with an opportunity to explore the dynamics of the process. Changes will inevitably occur, but as the researcher is able to isolate and describe phenomena he should be able to move toward a conceptualization of that phenomena that will help others to comprehend it. This holds true for comparative studies as well as for single-state studies. Without doubt problems multiply as the researcher moves beyond the relatively describable boundaries of a single-state policy-making system into the realm of multiple systems, but it is also at the latter level that there is the greatest potential benefit in the sense of usefulness. What is required is that the researcher look specifically for the similarities and differences between states to discover what, at the present level of understanding, must be assumed to be unique to particular states and what appears to be persistent across states. Iannaccone's typology described in Chapter 6 is one such effort.[14]

We believe that the systems framework is one of the most useful tools now available for describing and conceptualizing the interrelationships of actors and the flow of policy in the educational policy-making process. No claim is made that it can be used as a guide to the development of studies and the collection of data, but it does appear to be highly useful as a device for ordering findings and deriving general statements, especially statements of relationships, which can then be tested in other settings. The systems framework moves such exploration from the simple case description format so prevalent in political science to a level of analysis that is integrated, complete, and easily comprehended by others. Further, it is possible to test such conclusions against the realities of other state policy-making settings. In employing the systems framework it should be possible, as Wirt and Kirst note, "at least to order existing knowledge or hunches and thereby to determine what portions of the scheme are clearly untenable, which ones have at least some support, and which need to be further studied."[15] The systems concepts and visual models explored in the present chapter are examples of such uses of the systems framework. Exploring the findings of the study within the framework devised makes it possible to isolate tenable and untenable conclusions and move back into the policy-making arena to explicate the unknowns.

In short, it can be contended that the systems framework provides a vehicle that is dynamic in thrust and can be used to explain phenomena. There is a regularity in the behavior and the interaction patterns of the actors in the educational policy-making process, a process that analysts have just begun to explore with any semblance of organization. As the evidence mounts it should be feasible to move toward establishing conceptual frameworks that will provide guidance for analysis, for explanation, and possibly even for more accurate, though still highly tenable predictions of future actor behavior within the policy-making system.

The issue of whether education is an appropriate arena for the study of politics has finally been laid to rest. The debate has been settled as a result of thorough documentation by researchers that educators are engaged in political activity at all levels of government. Their competition with other government-sponsored areas for the allocation of scarce resources places them squarely in the middle of political activity. With this established it is important that policy researchers move from such rear-guard fire fighting toward the development of evidence and frameworks that will lead to clearer perceptions of interactions in the policy-making process. We hope that the present study has contributed in some small way to that goal.

CHAPTER 1

1. Harold Lasswell, Politics: Who Gets What, When, How (New York: McGraw-Hill 1936).

2. National Education Association, Financial Status of the Public Schools (Washington, D.C.: Committee on Educational Finance, 1971).

3. See, for example, Joseph Lincoln Steffens, The Shame of the Cities (New York: R. S. Smith, 1904).

4. Theodore W. Schultz, "Investment in Human Capital," American Economic Review, LI, 1 (March 1961), pp. 1-16.

5. Burton R. Clark, Educating the Expert Society (San Francisco: Chandler, 1962).

6. Laurence Iannaccone, Politics in Education (New York: Center for Applied Research in Education, 1967), p. 8.

7. National Education Association, op. cit.

8. National Education Association, Estimates of School Statistics, 1968-69 (Washington, D.C.: NEA Research Report 1968-R16, 1968), p. 18; National Education Association, Financial Status of the Public Schools, op. cit.

9. National Education Association, Schools for the 70's and Beyond: A Call to Action (Washington, D.C.: NEA 1971), p. 125.

10. National Education Association, Rankings of the States, 1960 (Washington, D.C.: NEA Research Division, 1960); National Education Association, Rankings of the States, 1970. (Washington, D.C.: NEA Research Division, 1970).

11. Iannaccone, op. cit.

12. Thomas H. Eliot, "Toward an Understanding of Public School Politics," American Political Science Review, LIII, 4 (December 1959), pp. 1032-1051.

13. Stephen K. Bailey et al., Schoolmen and Politics: A Study of State Aid to Education in the Northeast, "The Economics and Politics of Education Series," Vol. I (Syracuse, N.Y.: Syracuse University Press, 1962); Michael D. Usdan, The Political Power of Education in New York State (New York: Institute of Administrative Research, Teachers College, Columbia University, 1963); Nicholas A. Masters, Robert H. Salisbury and Thomas H. Eliot, State Politics and the Public Schools (New York: Alfred A. Knopf, 1964).

14. John C. Wahlke, Heinz Eulau, William Buchanan and LeRoy Ferguson, The Legislative System (New York: John Wiley

and Sons, 1962); LeRoy Ferguson, How State Legislators View the Problems of School Needs (U.S. Office of Education, Cooperative Research Project No. 532, 8116, 1960).

15. Lawrence J. Fahey, "The California Legislature and Educational Decision Making" (unpublished doctoral dissertation, Claremont Graduate School, 1958).

16. Tom Wiley, "State Politics and Educational Policy: A View From the Profession," Paper presented at the American Educational Research Association, Annual Conference, February 6, 1969.

17. Laurence Iannaccone, "The State and Educational Policy Formulation: Prospects for the Future," Paper presented at the American Educational Research Association, Annual Conference, February 6, 1969.

18. Baker v. Carr (1962) 369 U.S. 186.

19. Malcolm E. Jewell and Samuel C. Patterson, The Legislative Process in the United States (New York: Random House, 1966), p. 7.

20. Ibid., p. 6.

21. Wahlke et al., op. cit. See Chapter 18, pp. 435-463, "Strategy and Tactics of Legislative Research," for a detailed description of this survey process.

CHAPTER 2

1. David M. Ellis et al., A Short History of New York State (Ithaca, N.Y.: Cornell University Press, 1957), Chapter 36.

2. Ibid.

3. Frank J. Munger and Ralph A. Straetz, New York Politics (New York: New York University Press, 1960), pp. 1-4.

4. Stephen K. Bailey et al., Schoolmen and Politics: A Study of State Aid to Education in the Northeast, "The Economics and Politics of Education Series," Vol. I. Syracuse, N.Y.: Syracuse University Press, 1962), pp. 12-13.

5. Munger and Straetz, op. cit., pp. 41-50, 51-60.

6. Ellis et al., op. cit., pp. 589-592; Harlan H. Horner, ed., Education in New York State: 1754-1954 (Albany, N.Y.: University of the State of New York, State Education Department, 1954), pp. 12, 14.

7. State Education Department, Twenty-Fifth Annual Report of the State Education Department, II, 1929 (Albany, N.Y.: The University of the State of New York, 1930), p. 23; State Education Department, Twenty-Seventh Annual Report of the State Education Department, Vol. II, 1931 (Albany, N.Y.: The University of the State of New York, 1932), pp. 5, 24.

8. Robert E. Jennings, "An Historical Analysis of Organizational Change as a Function of Cooperative Activities of the New York State Teachers Association, 1904-1960" (unpublished Ed. D. dissertation, State University of New York at Albany, 1966), pp. 251-254.

9. Bailey et al., op. cit., pp. 32-33.

10. State Education Department, Federal Legislation and Education in New York State (Albany, N.Y.: The University of the State of New York, 1971), pp. 76, 82, 86; State Education Department, Federal Legislation and Education in New York State (Albany, N.Y.: The University of the State of New York, 1972), pp. 84, 82.

CHAPTER 3

1. Malcolm E. Jewell, The State Legislature: Politics and Practice (New York: Random House, 1962), pp. 9-11, 14-17.

2. David M. Ellis et al., A Short History of New York State (Ithaca, N.Y.: Cornell University Press, 1957), pp. 351-355, 388.

3. Jewell, op. cit., pp. 53-59.

4. Frank J. Munger and Ralph A. Straetz, New York Politics (New York: New York University Press, 1960), as quoted in Jewell, p. 55.

5. Robert Rienow, New York State and Local Government (2d rev. ed.; Albany, N.Y.: State Education Department, 1959), pp. 122-125.

6. John Burns, The Sometimes Governments: A Critical Study of the 50 American Legislatures (New York: Bantam Books, 1971), pp. 66-69.

7. Robert E. Jennings and Mike M. Milstein, "New York's Changing Educational Legislation Scene," The Quarterly, X (February 1969), pp. 47-49; Burns, op. cit., pp. 139-140.

8. Jewell, op. cit., pp. 14, 53-54.

9. Interview with Stanley Steingut, (D.-Brooklyn) Minority Leader in Assembly on "Capitol Report," WNED-TV, Buffalo, New York (January 14, 1969).

CHAPTER 4

1. Claudius O. Johnson, American State and Local Government, 3rd. ed. (New York: Thomas Y. Crowell, 1961), pp. 133-134.

2. David M. Ellis et al., A Short History of New York State (Ithaca, N.Y.: Cornell University Press, 1957), pp. 400-402.

3. Ibid.

4. Warren Moscow, Politics in the Empire State (New York: Alfred A. Knopf, 1948), pp. 77-81, 182-183.

5. Nicholas A. Masters, Robert H. Salisbury, and Thomas H. Eliot, State Politics and the Public Schools: An Exploratory Analysis (New York: Alfred A. Knopf, 1964), pp. 42-43, 166.

6. Stephen K. Bailey et al., Schoolmen and Politics: A Study of State Aid to Education in the Northeast, "The Economics and Politcs of Education Series," Vol. I (Syracuse, New York: Syracuse University Press, 1962), pp. 107-108.

7. James B. Conant, Shaping Educational Policy (New York: McGraw-Hill, 1964), p. 82.

8. Robert E. Jennings, Alternative Roles and Interagency Relationships of State Education Agencies in Comprehensive Statewide Planning. A report of a special study for the project Improving State Leadership in Education, Edgar L. Morphet, Project Director (Denver, Colo.: The Project, 1971), pp. 19-21.

9. Ibid.

CHAPTER 5

1. Edmund H. Crane et al., The New York State Education Department, 1900-65 (Albany, N.Y.: The State Education Department, The University of the State of New York, 1967).

2. Stephen K. Bailey et al., Schoolmen and Politics: A Study of State Aid to Education in the Northeast, "The Economics and Politics of Education Series," Vol. I (Syracuse, N.Y.: Syracuse University Press, 1962), p. 27.

3. Arvis Chalmers, Albany Has Its Pentagon: State Education Department (Albany, N.Y.: n.p., 1968) (mimeographed), pp. 1-4. Chalmers was the Capitol reporter for the Albany Knickerbocker News.

4. Division of Educational Finance, State Aid for Elementary and Secondary Education in New York State as Apportioned in 1969-70. (Albany, N.Y.: State Education Department), 1971, pp. 1-9; State Education Department, Major Recommendations of the Regents for Legislative Action, 1972. (Albany, N.Y.: The University of the State of New York, 1971), pp. 64-68.

5. John F. Brosnan, Regent of the University, A State Board of Education in Action. (Albany, N.Y.: The Regents of the University, 1965).

6. James B. Conant, Shaping Educational Policy (New York: McGraw-Hill, 1964), pp. 86-90.

7. The Regents' Inquiry, Education for American Life: A New Program for the State of New York (New York: McGraw-Hill, 1938).

8. State Education Department, Major Recommendations of the State Board of Regents for Legislative Action, 1969. (Albany, N.Y.: The University of the State of New York, 1968), p. 20.

9. Robert D. Samberg, "Conceptualization and Measurement of Political System Output: Decisions Within Issue Contexts" (unpublished Ph.D. dissertation, University of Rochester, 1971), pp. 503-508.

10. Belle Zeller, Pressure Politics in New York State (New York: Prentice-Hall, 1937), pp. 156-158; Bailey et al., op cit., pp. 36-37, 59-61; Robert E. Jennings, "An Historical Analysis of Organizational Change as a Function of Cooperative Activities of the New York State Teachers Association, 1904-1960" (unpublished Ed. D. dissertation, State University of New York at Albany, 1966), pp. 199-202, 268-270.

11. Conant, op. cit., pp. 31-33.

12. Jennings, op. cit., pp. 109-114.

CHAPTER 6

1. Charles E. Lindblom, The Policy-Making Process (Englewood Cliffs, N.J.: Prentice-Hall, 1968).

2. Gabriel A. Almond and G. Bingham Powell, Jr., Comparative Politics (Boston: Little, Brown, 1966).

3. Wallace S. Sayre and Herbert Kaufman, Governing New York City (New York: W. W. Norton, 1960).

4. Ibid., p. 78.

5. Ibid., p. 79.

6. Stephen K. Bailey et al., Schoolmen and Politics: A Study of State Aid to Education in the Northeast, "The Economics and Politics of Education Series," Vol. I (Syracuse, N.Y.: Syracuse University Press, 1962).

7. Michael D. Usdan, "The Political Power of Education in New York State: A Second Look," Presentation made at the Sixteenth Annual Summer Work Conference of the Central School Boards Committee for Educational Research at Randolph House, Syracuse, New York, June 4, 1967. By permission of the author.

8. Ibid., p. 13.

9. John Wahlke et al., The Legislative System: Explorations in Legislative Behavior (New York: Wiley, 1962), p. 338.

10. State Education Department, University of the State of New York, "Education Statistics Estimates, Fall 1971" (Albany, N.Y.: Information Center on Education, State Education Department, fall 1971).

11. For further exploration of this phenomenon, see Robert E. Jennings, "An Historical Analysis of Organizational Change as a Function of Cooperative Activities of the New York State Teachers Association, 1904-1960" (unpublished Ed.D. dissertation, State University of New York at Albany, 1966).

12. This view of membership as opposed to leader effectiveness as interest group influencing mechanisms is confirmed in a
recent four state study by Zeigler and Baer. See Harmon Zeigler
and Michael Baer, Lobbying: Interaction and Influence in American
State Legislatures (Belmont, Calif.: Wadsworth, 1969).
13. Heinz Eulau, The Behavioral Persuasion in Politics
(New York: Random House, 1963), pp. 54-60.

CHAPTER 7
1. Stephen K. Bailey et al., Schoolmen and Politics: A Study
of State Aid to Education in the Northeast "The Economics and
Politics of Education Series," Vol. I (Syracuse, N.Y.: Syracuse
University Press, 1962), pp. 32-33.
2. The Executive Department, State of New York Annual
Message, 1969-70, Nelson A. Rockefeller, Governor (Albany,
N.Y.: The Department, 1969), pp. m18, m38-m39.
3. State Education Department, Major Recommendations
of the State Board of Regents for Legislative Action, 1969 (Albany,
N.Y.: The University of the State of New York, 1968), pp. 5-7, 20.
4. Interview with Stanley Steingut, (D.-Brooklyn) Minority
Leader in Assembly, on "Capitol Report," WNED-TV, Buffalo,
New York (January 14, 1969).
5. New York State Educational Conference Board, Education
for the Seventies: A Review of Public School Finance, 1969-70.
(Albany, N.Y.: The Conference Board, 1969). The study was not
released until September 1969.
6. NYSTA News Trends, February 1969, p. 1; NYSTA news
release, February 12, 1969.
7. State of New York, The Assembly, Message to the
Legislature, Nelson A. Rockefeller, Governor, Legislative
Document No. 1, 1969, pp. 28-29.
8. Report of the New York State Commission on the
Quality, Cost and Financing of Elementary and Secondary Education
in New York State, I (Albany, N.Y.: The Commission, 1972), pp.
2.12-2.16, 4.10-4.11, 5.2.
9. John F, McGowan, "Legislature Focus on Education,"
Central Ideas, XXIII, September 1972, pp. 1-4; Buffalo Evening
News, September 9, 1972.
10. The University of the State of New York, The State
Education Department, Home Rule Education Bill, Memorandum
to the Legislature, February 14, 1971; Bureau of School and
Cultural Research, Historical Review of Studies and Proposals
Relative to Decentralization of Administration in the New York
City Public School System (Albany, N.Y.: State Education Depart-
ment, 1967).

11. Commissioner's Advisory Commission on Human Relations and Community Tensions, Desegregating the Public Schools of New York City, A Report for the Board of Education of the City of New York (Albany, N.Y.: State Education Department, 1964).

12. Ibid.

13. Mayor's Advisory Panel on Decentralization of the New York City Schools, McGeorge Bundy, Chairman, Reconnection for Learning (New York: Praeger, 1969).

14. Fred Hechinger, New York Times, May 14, 1965, p. 1; Fred Hechinger, "New Schools," New York Times, October 4, 1967.

15. New York City Board of Education, "Plans for Development of a Community School District System for the City of New York," (New York: The Board of Education, 1969); State Education Department, "Recommendations of the Board of Regents Concerning a Plan for the Development of a Community School District System for the City of New York Submitted by the New York City School Board of Education," (Albany, N.Y.: The University of the State of New York, 1969).

16. New York Times, May 4, 1969, p. C3.

17. Ibid.

18. Ibid.

CHAPTER 8

1. John C. Wahlke et al., The Legislative System: Explorations in Legislative Behavior (New York: Wiley, 1962).

2. John Burns, The Sometime Governments: A Critical Case Study of the Fifty American Legislatures (New York: Bantam Books, 1971), p. 52.

3. Gabriel A. Almond and G. Bingham Powell, Jr., Comparative Politics (Boston: Little, Brown, 1966).

4. Wallace S. Sayre and Herbert Kaufman, Governing New York City: Politics in the Metropolis (New York: W. W. Norton, 1960).

5. Laurence Iannaccone, Politics in Education (New York: Center for Applied Research in Education, 1967).

6. Heinz Eulau, The Behavioral Persuasion in Politics. (New York: Random House, 1963).

7. David Easton, "Categories for the Systems Analysis of Politics," in David Easton, ed., Varieties of Political Theory (Englewood Cliffs, New Jersey: Prentice-Hall, 1966), p. 145.

8. Mike M. Milstein, "Organization of the California State Education Department to Administer Two Federal Education Programs," Education, XCI, 2 (November-December 1970), p. 117.

9. Michael W. Kirst and Edith K. Mosher, "Politics of Education," Review of Educational Research, XXXIX, 5 (December 1969), p. 629.

10. Gerald Sroufe, "Political Systems Analysis in Educational Administration: Can the Emperor be Clothed?" Paper presented at the American Educational Research Association, Annual Conference, February 1969.

11. Iannaccone, op. cit., p. 81.

12. Frederick M. Wirt and Michael W. Kirst, The Political Web of American Schools. (Boston: Little, Brown, 1972), p. 145.

13. Stephen K. Bailey et al., Schoolmen and Politics: A Study of State Aid to Education in the Northeast "The Economics and Politics of Education Series," Vol. I (Syracuse, New York: Syracuse University Press, 1962): Nicholas A. Masters, Robert H. Salisbury and Thomas A. Eliot, State Politics and the Public Schools: An Exploratory Analysis. (New York: Alfred A. Knopf, 1964); Iannaccone, op. cit.

14. Iannaccone, op. cit.

15. Wirt and Kirst, op. cit., p. 13.

Abbott, Frank C. Government Policy and Higher Education: A Study of the Regents of the University of the State of New York, 1784-1949. Ithaca, New York: Cornell University Press, 1958.

Almond, Gabriel A., and G. Bingham Powell, Jr. Comparative Politics. Boston: Little, Brown. 1966.

Bailey, Stephen K., et al. Schoolmen and Politics: A Study of State Aid to Education in the Northeast. "The Economics and Politics of Education Series," Vol. I. Syracuse, New York: Syracuse University Press, 1962.

Bendiner, Robert. The Politics of Schools. New York: Harper and Row, 1969.

Bloomburg, Warner, Jr., and Morris Sunshine. Suburban Power Structures and Public Education: A Study of Values, Influence and Tax Effort. "The Economics and Politics of Education Series," Vol. X. Syracuse, New York: Syracuse University Press, 1963.

Brosnan, John F., Regent of the University. A State Board of Education in Action. Albany, New York: The Regents of the University, 1955.

Burns, John. The Sometimes Governments: A Critical Study of the 50 American Legislatures. New York: Bantam Books, 1971.

Caldwell, Lynton K. The Government and Administration of New York. New York: Thomas Y. Crowell, 1954.

Clark, Burton R. Educating the Expert Society. San Francisco: Chandler, 1962.

Cohen, Sol. Progressives and Urban School Reform: The Public Education Association of New York City, 1895-1954. New York: Bureau of Publications, Teachers College, Columbia University, 1963.

Conant, James B. Shaping Educational Policy. New York: McGraw-Hill, 1964.

Crane, Edmund H., et al. The New York State Education Department, 1900-65. Albany, New York: The State Education Department, The University of the State of New York, 1967.

Dahl, Robert A. Modern Political Analysis. Englewood Cliffs, New Jersey: Prentice-Hall, 1963.

Easton, David, ed. Varieties of Political Theory. Englewood Cliffs, New Jersey: Prentice-Hall, 1966.

Eliot, Thomas A. "Toward an Understanding of Public School Politics," American Political Science Review, LIII 4 (December 1959), 1032-1051.

Ellis, David M., et al. A History of New York State. Ithaca, New York: Cornell University Press, 1967.

Eulau, Heinz. The Behavioral Persuasion in Politics. New York: Random House, 1963.

Fahey, Lawrence J. "The California Legislature and Educational Decision Making." Unpublished dissertation, Claremont Graduate School, 1958.

Ferguson, LeRoy C. How State Legislators View the Problem of School Needs. USOE, DHEW, Cooperative Research Project No. 532 (8166), 1960. Mimeographed.

Graves, Frank P. History of the New York State Education Department. Albany, New York: The University of the State of New York, 1941.

Hodge, D. Emma Wilber, and Lamont Foster Hodge. A Century of Service to Public Education. Albany, New York: New York State Teachers Association, 1945.

Horner, Harlan H., ed. Education in New York State: 1784-1954. Albany, New York: The University of the State of New York, State Education Department, 1954.

Iannaccone, Laurence. Politics in Education. New York: Center for Applied Research in Education, Inc., 1967.

_____. "The State and Educational Policy Formulation: Prospects for the Future." Paper presented at the American Educational Research Association, Annual Conference, February 1964.

Jennings, Robert E. Alternative Roles and Interagency Relationships of State Education Agencies in Comprehensive State-Wide Planning. A report of a special study for the project Improving State Leadership in Education, Edgar L. Morphet, Project Director. Denver, Colorado: The Project, 1971.

_____. "An Historical Analysis of Organizational Change as a Function of Cooperative Activities of the New York State Teachers Association, 1904-1960." Unpublished Ed.D. dissertation, State University of New York at Albany, 1966.

_____ and Mike M. Milstein. Educational Policy Making in New York State with Emphasis on the Role of the State Legislature. U.S. Office of Education, Small Grants Project No. 9-8-030, December 1970.

_____. "New York's Changing Educational Legislation Scene," The Quarterly, X (February, 1969), 47-49.

Jewell, Malcolm E. The State Legislature: Politics and Practice. New York: Random House, 1962.

Jewell, Malcolm E., and Samuel C. Patterson. The Legislative Process in the United States. New York: Random House, 1966.

Johnson, Claudius O. American State and Local Government. Third edition. New York: Thomas Y. Crowell, 1961.

Kaufman, Herbert. Politics and Policies in State and Local Governments. Englewood Cliffs, New Jersey: Prentice-Hall, 1963.

Kirst, Michael W., and Edith K. Mosher. "Politics of Education," Review of Educational Research, XXXIX, 5 (December 1969), 623-640.

Lasswell, Harold. Politics: Who Gets What, When, How. New York: McGraw-Hill, 1936.

Lindblom, Charles E. The Policy-Making Process. Englewood Cliffs, New Jersey: Prentice-Hall, 1968.

MacIver, Robert M. The Web of Government. New York: MacMillan, 1947.

Martin, Roscoe C. Government and the Suburban School. "The Economics and Politics of Education Series," Vol. II. Syracuse, New York: Syracuse University Press, 1962.

Masters, Nicholas A., Robert H. Salisbury, and Thomas H. Eliot. State Politics and the Public Schools: An Exploratory Analysis. New York: Alfred A. Knopf, 1964.

Milstein, Mike M. "Organization of the California State Education Department to Administer Two Federal Education Programs," Education, XCI, 2 (November-December 1970), 117-126.

Moscow, Warren. Politics in the Empire State. New York: Alfred A. Knopf, 1948.

Munger, Frank J., and Ralph A. Straetz. New York Politics. New York: New York University Press, 1960.

National Education Association. Schools for the 70's and Beyond: A Call to Action. Washington, D.C.: National Education Association, 1971.

Reinow, Robert. New York State and Local Government. Second revised edition. Albany, New York: State Education Department, 1959.

Roberts, Steven V. "Prospects for New York's Conservatives," New Leader, XLIX (December 19, 1966), 14-16.

Rogers, David. 110 Livingston Street. New York: Random House, 1968.

Rosenberg, Bernard. "New York Politics and the Liberal Party," Commentary, XXXVII (February 1964), 69-75.

Samberg, Robert D. "Conceptualization and Measurement of Political System Output: Decisions Within Issue-Contexts." Unpublished Ph.D. dissertation, University of Rochester, 1971.

Sayre, Wallace S., and Herbert Kaufman. Governing New York City: Politics in the Metropolis. New York: W. W. Norton, Inc., 1960.

Schultz, Theodore W., "Investment in Human Capital," American Economic Review, LI, 1 (March 1961), 1-16.

Sroufe, Gerald. "Political Systems Analysis in Educational Administration: Can the Emperor be Clothed?" Paper presented at the American Educational Research Association, Annual Conference, February 1969.

Truman, David B. The Governmental Process. New York: Alfred A. Knopf, 1957.

Usdan, Michael D. The Political Power of Education in New York State. New York: Institute of Administrative Research, Columbia University, 1963.

_____. "The Political Power of Education in New York State: A Second Look." A paper presented at the 16th Annual Summer Work Conference of the Central School Boards Committee for Research, Syracuse, New York, June 4, 1967.

_____. "The Role and Future of State Education Coalitions," Educational Administration Quarterly (Spring, 1969), 27-41.

Usdan, Michael D., David W. Minar and Emanuel Hurwitz, Jr. Education and State Politics: The Developing Relationship Between Elementary, Secondary and Higher Education. New York: Teachers College Press, 1969.

Wahlke, John C., et al. The Legislative System: Explorations in Legislative Behavior. New York: Wiley, 1962.

Wiley, Tom. "State Politics and Educational Policy: A View From the Profession." Paper presented at the American Educational Research Association, Annual Conference, February 1969.

Wirt, Frederick M., and Michael W. Kirst. The Political Web of American Schools. Boston: Little, Brown, 1972.

Wootton, Graham. Interest Groups. Englewood Cliffs, New Jersey: Prentice-Hall, 1970.

Zeigler, Harmon, and Michael Baer. Lobbying: Interaction and Influence in American State Legislatures. Belmont, California: Wadsworth, 1969.

Zeller, Belle. Pressure Politics in New York. New York: Prentice-Hall, 1937.

12, 31; and staff 65-69, 127; (see also Democrats, Dewey, Thomas E., Governor, Harriman, W. Averell, Governor, Republicans, Rockefeller, Nelson D., Governor

Harriman, W. Averell, Governor 61
Heck, Oswald, Speaker of the Assembly 52, 60

Iannaccone, Laurence 4, 8, 88, 129, 139
Influence Sources: Board of Regents 55; executive department agencies 54, 57; governor 55; interest groups 55, 57, 93-98, 102, 103-104; legislature 55; State Education Department 55; voters 55
Information: control 92-93; sources 52-54, 76, 126; use of 53, 101-102
Interest groups: and blacks 116-117, 120; and Board of Regents 98; and governor 95, 98, 99; and influence 54-55, 92-98, 102-104, 130; and legislature 98, 99-100, 100-101, 103; and policy making 98-100, 101-102, 104-105, 129-130, 134, 136-137; role 6-7, 9-10, 12; structure 81-83, 83, 88; (see also Big Five Cities, Educational Conference Board, New York Council of School District Administrators, New York State School Boards Association, New York State Teachers Association, United Federation of Teachers, United Teachers of New York)

Jewell, Malcolm E. 9, 34, 35
Johnson, Claudius O. 58
Joint Legislative Committees (JLC's) 48; Diefendorf Committee

107; JLC to Revise and Simplify the Education Law 48, 107, 108, 113

Kaufman, Herbert 83

Legislative committees 39, 51; Education Committee 48, 51, 95; Finance, Senate 39, 51, 110, 126; Rules, Assembly 38, 39, 125; Rules, Senate 38, 39, 125-126; Ways and Means, Assembly 39, 51, 53-54, 110, 126; (see also Joint Legislative Committees)
Legislative leadership: legislators' perceptions of 40, 42, 50; minority leaders 43, 59, 61, 70, 95, 120; Senate Majority Leader 37, 38-39, 40, 44, 48, 51, 53, 60, 122, 126; Speaker of the Assembly 37, 38-39, 40, 44, 51, 60, 126
Legislature: and Board of Regents 77-78; and decentralization 115, 117, 119-120, 122, 123; and education 46-47, 50-51; and governor 44-45, 61-65, 69-70; and interest groups 100, 100-101; and partisanship 43-44; party control of 34-35; perceptions of 35, 37, 42, 43, 44, 49-50, 55, 99-100, 101-102, 103-105, 130, 135; and policy making process 50-51, 98, 134, 135-137; powers 33-35; as processing system 125-126, 129; role 12, 13; and state aid 112, 114, 123

Lehman, Herbert A., Governor 19, 63
Liberal Party 22, 23
Lindsay, John, Mayor of New York City 117, 118

Marchi, John, Senator 118, 120, 121

ABOUT THE AUTHORS

MIKE M. MILSTEIN Associate Professor, Department of Educational Administration, State University of New York at Buffalo, has evidenced a long and continuing interest in educational policy-making. He has written extensively in this area and has served as chairman of the American Educational Research Association's Special Interest Group on the Politics of Education. Dr. Milstein received his doctorate in education from the University of California at Berkeley.

ROBERT E. JENNINGS, Assistant Professor, Department of Educational Administration, State University of New York at Buffalo, specializes in the study of state and local politics of education. He has written articles on many topics in education and politics including planning curriculum as well as state policy-making. One of his monographs focuses on interagency relationships in state-wide planning. Professor Jennings received his doctorate in education from the State University of New York at Albany.

POLITICAL FEASIBILITY OF REFORM
IN SCHOOL FINANCING

Meltser, Kast, Kramer, Nakamura

SCHOOL BOARDS AND SCHOOL POLICY

Marilyn Gittell

THE URBAN EDUCATION TASK FORCE REPORT

Wilson C. Riles